Paul Galloway has worked as a copy-writer, journalist, publicist, dramaturg and playwright. He currently writes and edits Melbourne Theatre Company publications. From 1995 to 2002, he wrote a weekly theatre column for *Brisbane News*. He has also written for the *Bulletin*, the *Courier-Mail* and the *Age*. His play *Great Leaders of the Twentieth Century* won the 2001 QTC/Courier-Mail George Landan Dann Award and was subsequently presented in a rehearsed reading at the 2001 Brisbane Writers' Festival. In 2002, his play, *Low Sunday*, about the anti-Nazi theologian Dietrich Bonhoeffer, was presented as part of Brisbane's Cathedrals Week. *Realism* was short-listed for the 2007 Patrick White Award and won the Wal Cherry Award in 2008. Galloway was co-founder of ACRONYM Theatre Company and directed their productions of *The Visit*, *King Lear*, *Too Clever by Half*, *As You Like It*, *Teechers*, *Cyrano de Bergerac*, *A Place with the Pigs* and *Bent*.

REALISM

PAUL GALLOWAY

CURRENCY PRESS

CURRENCY PLAYS

First published in 2009
by Currency Press Pty Ltd,
PO Box 2287, Strawberry Hills, NSW, 2012, Australia
enquiries@currency.com.au
www.currency.com.au
in association with
Melbourne Theatre Company

Reprinted in 2014

NATIONAL LIBRARY OF AUSTRALIA CIP DATA

Author: Galloway, Paul, 1961–.
Title: Realism / Paul Galloway.
ISBN: 9780868198521 (pbk.).
Target Audience: For secondary school age.
Dewey Number: A822.4

Typeset by Dean Nottle for Currency Press.
Front cover shows Stephen Phillips and Miriam Margolyes in Melbourne
Theatre Company's production of Realism. Photo: Earl Carter.
Cover design by Laura McLean, Currency Press.

Currency Press acknowledges the Traditional Owners of the Country on which
we live and work. We pay our respects to all Aboriginal and Torres Strait
Islander Elders, past and present.

Contents

For Ruth,
a poor reward for her patience

INTRODUCTION

I must have heard the nightmare tale of Meyerhold's persecution and execution while studying drama at university twenty years ago. It's also likely that I learnt then about the death of his wife, the actress Zinaida Raikh, horribly murdered by 'thugs' in her apartment a few weeks after Meyerhold's arrest in the summer of 1939. Yet these horrors made little impression on me at the time. Meyerhold was very much a peripheral figure in theatre theory in the late-eighties. If he was spoken of at all, it was only as a major influence on Brecht and the artistic rival of Stanislavski. A tag of 'genius' had accrued to his reputation, but little evidence was brought forth to substantiate it. We were told that he invented a training system called 'biomechanics', for which there were ambiguous descriptions and a few unhelpful photos, and that these exercises somehow fed into his work for the stage in the first decade or so after the Bolshevik Revolution. The photos of these productions—*Mystery Bouffe*, *The Bedbug*, *The Forest*, *The Bathhouse*, *The Government Inspector* and *The Magnanimous Cuckold*—still had the power to cause wonder, with their constructivist settings and expressionistic poses. But the details that would have given life to the figure and work of Meyerhold were lost with his arrest and subsequent erasure from the official Soviet histories.

That all changed with the collapse of communism and the opening up of the Soviet archives. In the mid-nineties I read the revised edition of Edward Braun's biography and dramaturgical study, *Meyerhold: A Revolution in Theatre*, which incorporated a great deal of this new material, including extracts from his police file. One item in particular made pitiful reading: Meyerhold's pleading letter to the authorities detailing his interrogation and torture. By the time he wrote it his wife had been murdered, and one can only hope that his torturers at least extended the mercy of not telling him about it before putting him to death.

The double shock of realising the substance of Meyerhold's achievement at the same time as grasping the enormity of his persecution and State-sanctioned murder led to my writing *Realism*. The play, however, was slow in gestation and developed differently from my initial idea of a play of Meyerhold's life as Meyerhold might have produced it (though this idea, as you see, is retained in the last ten minutes of *Realism*). As I began to read more deeply into the history of the Stalinist purges of the thirties, especially as it affected the arts, it became clear that Meyerhold's was an atypical case. He was big enough and important enough to resist, to answer back to power and to struggle for his art, even if, by the end, the struggle assumed the futility of an insect squirming on a pin. More typical was the silencing of a generation of literary talent that any sane society would have cherished: Osip Mandelstam, Anna Akhmatova, Maria Tsvetaeva, Boris Pasternak, Nicolai Erdman, Yuri Olesha and Mikhail Bulgakov—to allow the names of the most outstanding to represent the many.

Easily, the most common reaction to Stalinist regulation of culture was acquiescence. Artists relied completely on the State for their livelihoods and did what they had to do to keep their jobs. In literature and drama, Socialist Realism became the official and mandatory form, and it favoured hacks, those with talent large enough to make a living but not large enough to push against the limitations. In music, experimentation was dropped in favour of safety, as when Shostakovich buckled under attacks on his opera *Lady Macbeth* in Mtensk with a Fifth Symphony cringingly subtitled: 'A Soviet artist's response to just criticism'. Theatre and film directors sometimes criticised policy within the narrow, officially-tolerated bounds of debate, but no-one came close to Meyerhold's persistent dissent. Actors generally accepted the stereotyped roles in the 'tractor romances' they were given and kept quiet. When one actor, Shinin, cried out during a theatre conference discussion, 'Stop feeding us Soviet straw!', he effectively booked his passage to a gulag.

The more I read about conditions in the Soviet Union in the thirties the more I realised that a play that caught the spirit of that terrifying decade had to be a comedy—a black comedy, admittedly, but not a tragedy. For the story of overwhelming power crushing ordinary people is structurally a comic one. Tragedy requires that the hero could have avoided his fate by acting differently. In the Soviet Union under Stalin acting differently would have had little effect and was likely to make things worse. Soviet artists, like large sections of Soviet society, could only avoid imprisonment or death by keeping their heads down and their fingers crossed. Fear ruled their lives and kept their actions in check. When Bergson theorised that comedy arises when human beings are forced to behave like machines, he got Soviet society in one.

In *Realism*, I placed fundamentally comic characters in a fearful situation and slowly increased the fear, making them at first funnier and then, as their histories are revealed, more human. At first glance, the characters seem timeless theatre types: a cocky juvenile lead, a feisty ingénue, a doyenne, a classical actor, a character actor, a nervy writer and a stern stage manager. I have met real examples of all these people in my years in the theatre and their allotropes were clearly recognisable in the accounts I read of theatre life in Russia and the Soviet Union. In creating them, I tried to capture the slightly overblown characterisation of popular nineteenth-century comedies, particularly those by Ostrovsky. Kamev and Dinsky are first cousins to the two fatuous out-of-work thespians in Ostrovsky's *The Forest*, Nadia could be any one of Ostrovsky's dowagers, and Klimenko lives according to the go-getter ethos of Glumov in *Even a Wise Man Stumbles*. As a final tip of the hat, I gave the ending of *Realism* a strong echo of the ending of Russia's greatest comedy, Gogol's *The Government Inspector*.

Placing these broad Ostrovskian figures into the straitened reality of Stalinist Moscow was, therefore, the central conceit of the play. I have always tried to keep the historical milieu as close to reality as possible. To keep me honest, I affixed to the front page of my first drafts a quote from Henry James's *The Aspern Papers*: 'The historian, essentially, wants more documents than he can really use; the dramatist only wants more liberties than he can really take.' Thus,

I tried hard not to take liberties with the history, while not allowing the facts to cramp my invention. All the stated details about Meyerhold's arrest and Raikh's murder are accurate, as are the names and places in the Civil War in the rehearsed play *Man of Steel*. Similarly, I did my best—the best a well-fed Australian writer seventy years later could manage—to give a sense of the privations of life in Moscow in the thirties: the endless shortages, the queuing, the cramped and cruddy apartments and, of course, the pervasive and unrelenting fear. Through the entire writing process, including a workshop and two readings, I aspired to Marianne Moore's famous line about poets creating 'imaginary gardens with real toads in them'; though, perhaps, in the case of *Realism*, that should be inverted: my toads are harmless but imaginary, while the garden I dropped them in was dangerous and real.

Thanks

Writing for the stage is never a lone enterprise. Many people must get involved if a script has a chance of finding an audience. So I would like to thank those who helped me to get the play to this point: early enthusiasts and supporters—Kate Shearer (who loved the idea of the play long before a word was written); Marie Lynagh, Paul Denny and Bec Denny; the actors who gave their energy, enthusiasm and suggestions at the first workshop at MTC in February 2008—Tyler Coppin, Daniel Frederiksen, Bojana Novakovic, Deidre Rubenstein, Tony Taylor, Maria Theodorakis and Ashley Zuckerman; Tiffany Noack; the actors in the Wal Cherry Award reading—Nicholas Bell, Sara Gleeson, Grant Piro, Stephen Phillips, Julie Eckersley, James Saunders and David Tredinnick; Co-Artistic Director of STC Andrew Upton, who brought the play to the attention of MTC; and former STC Artistic Director Robyn Nevin. I would like give special thanks to MTC Artistic Director Simon Phillips and General Manager Ann Tonks for having faith in the play and overcoming their understandable qualms about producing a show written by an employee of the Company. Writing this before rehearsals of the premiere production,

I cannot know what specific effects the dedication and expertise of the cast, creative team, crew and MTC staff will have on the final production, but I thank them in advance for giving it every chance of success. Finally, I would like to thank Nigel Poulton, who opened my eyes to what biomechanics really meant (and thus precipitated a frantic rewrite), and Peter Evans, who always knew exactly what was wrong with the early drafts and didn't stop badgering me until we had the best play my talents could produce.

Paul Galloway
January 2009

Realism was first produced by Melbourne Theatre Company at the Sumner Theatre, Melbourne, on 4 April 2009, with the following cast:

KLIMENKO	Paul Denny
MOKHOVA	Julie Eckersley
BABELEV	John Leary
KAMEV	Tony Llewellyn-Jones
NADIA	Miriam Margolyes
GLEMOV	Stephen Phillips
DINSKY	Grant Piro
YAKONOVA	Ming-Zhu Hii
TRIFINOV	Mark Constable

Director, Peter Evans
Set Designer, Stephen Curtis
Lighting Designer, Matt Scott
Choreographer, Nick Poulton
Assistant Director, Mark Constable
Costume Designer, Christina Smith
Composer, Ian McDonald

CHARACTERS

GLEMOV, footballer, male, 20s
MOKHOVA, stage manager, female, late 20s
NADIA, actor, female, elderly
KLIMENKO, actor, male, 30s
KAMEV, actor, male, 50s
DINSKY, actor, male, 40s
BABELEV, playwright, male, 30s
YAKONOVA, actor, female, early 20s
TRIFINOV, director, male, late 30s

SETTING

A theatre in Moscow in 1939.

ACT ONE

The stage of a small, rundown theatre in Moscow.

The stage is set for a play called Precision Milled. *The flats and/or flies are mismatched, skewed with large gaps between them, an indication that the scene shifters began to prepare for the next performance but had stopped halfway.*

To the right and upstage is the refectory of a Soviet factory with a double-swing glass panelled door upstage centre. A long refectory table, surrounded by a number of incongruous 'prop' chairs from various productions, is set for the day's rehearsal. Also a stage manager's lectern with prompt book.

The left stage flat belongs to the factory itself—brickwork, pipes, work benches, etcetera. High on the wall, a prominent portrait of Stalin and a Stalinist slogan in big red letters: 'LIFE HAS BECOME BETTER. LIFE HAS BECOME MORE CHEERFUL'.

There is a door downstage left. Also downstage left is a metalworker's lathe, hooked up to a chain, with a block and tackle, disappearing into the fly space.

It is the morning of Saturday the fifteenth of July 1939, a warm summer's day.

The play begins. A face appears in the glass panelling of the rear doors, looking around tentatively. The doors are pushed open. It is GLEB EGOROVICH GLEMOV, *thirty, tall, strong, clean-shaven, a plaster cast on his left wrist, carrying a playscript.*

GLEMOV: Hello?

> *No reply. He wanders the stage looking around.*

Hello?

> *He examines the lathe and gives it a hearty slap. It sounds hollow. Perplexed, he gives it a push and it rocks easily—plywood and paint. But as he rocks it, the hook, chain and tackle swing loose*

across the stage. He chases it, has some difficulty catching it, before swinging it back to attach to the lathe. But now it won't attach. Eventually, in a mild panic, he hooks it onto the front edge of the set and walks as far away from it as possible.

Now at the edge of the stage, he looks out into the darkness.

Hello? Anyone there? [*Pause.*] Anyone? [*He likes the echo.*] I see. I understand. [*Pause.*] I must be audible to the back of the stalls. I project my voice. The voice is my most valuable, val-u-a-ble, in-strum-ment. Are you copper bottoming 'em, my man? No, I'm aluminimim—no I'm alumimimiming—No, I'm alu-min-ium-ing 'em, ma'am. Are you copper bomming—Are you cobber potting. Are you—?

He hears something. He creeps upstage listening. He looks through the door into the darkness.

Anyone there? [*Pause.*] Hello?

No reply. He returns downstage and pulls out a prop pipe. As he speaks, SOPHIA LEONIDOVNA MOKHOVA, *the stage manager, severe, late twenties, appears at the rear carrying a jug of water and a stack of glasses. She stops for a second and takes him in. She places the jug and glasses on the table.*

[*In a more actorly style with a bad accent, imitating Stalin*] You know who I am, don't you? Look at this moustache. Look at this pipe. Listen to this fine Georgian accent that is now projecting to the back of the stalls. All Soviet peoples must project to the back of the stalls. Comrades! In my big Georgian hand I carry the latest five-year plan, a blueprint, no, a red print for the future. We will carry out this five-year plan no matter how long it takes. For we are building a radiant Soviet Union...

He stops, listens. MOKHOVA *exits.* GLEMOV *turns.*

Hello?

Nobody; so he continues. During the following speech MOKHOVA *re-enters carrying a tall stool. She places it by the lectern and sits, folding her arms to glumly watch the performance.*

For we are building a radiant Soviet Union, a great and glorious and radiant and luscious and really nice Union of Soviet peoples in which we are all brothers in arms, sisters in suffering, mothers of invention and Jacks of all trades. Now to celebrate this glorious and radiant five-year plan I will whistle an old Georgian tune while doing that funny thing with my knees.

He starts whistling and passing his swinging knees from hand to hand, Charleston style. As he does so, he senses MOKHOVA'S *presence and, while still doing the dance, turns to look upstage. Seeing nothing, he turns back.*

MOKHOVA: [*clapping her hands officiously*] Comrade!

GLEMOV: [*jumping out of his skin*] Oh, God!

MOKHOVA: What are you doing?

GLEMOV: The funny knee thing.

MOKHOVA: No today, Comrade. You have not been called for today.

GLEMOV: Yes—

MOKHOVA: We're not starting your scenes until Wednesday.

GLEMOV: Yes, I know—

MOKHOVA: You must keep to the schedule, Comrade.

GLEMOV: Yes, but the woman in the flat below me cooks cabbage and, you see, when—

MOKHOVA: That sounds like the beginning of a brilliant explanation, Comrade, but you must leave. They are the rules.

GLEMOV: Sophia Leonidovna.

MOKHOVA *gives him a withering glare.*

Sorry… Comrade. I'm new to the theatre, as you know, and I would just like to sit in, if I may.

MOKHOVA: You may not.

GLEMOV: Just to see what's involved.

MOKHOVA: It's not complicated. Actors do it. Now, please—

GLEMOV: [*pointing to the stalls*] I could watch from that seat there…

Her expression is not encouraging.

Or one even further back, way back, in the dark…

MOKHOVA: Comrade, you are trying my patience.

GLEMOV: Listen, no, listen. I'll square it with Comrade Trifinov—

MOKHOVA: [*coming down hard, clapping her hands*] No. Comrade Glemov, get one thing straight and get it straight now, because otherwise your career in the theatre is going to be very short. I am stage manager—

GLEMOV: I know—

MOKHOVA: Shut up. Everyone sticks to my schedule.

GLEMOV: But Comrade Trifinov—

MOKHOVA: Comrade Trifinov is only the director. He has his name on the poster and gets to call himself an artist. But everyone in the theatre calls themselves an artist, artists are fifty to the kopek. But, Comrade, there is only one stage manager, and everyone, including Comrade Trifinov, follows my schedule. Do I make myself clear?

> *Enter* YURI KLIMENKO, *thirty-ish, a breezy, smart-arse manner, a Ukrainian actor.*

KLIMENKO: Be careful how you answer, chum.

MOKHOVA: Comrade, you are five minutes late.

KLIMENKO: Oh, I'm sorry! Is everybody waiting for me?

MOKHOVA: No, in fact you are the first—

KLIMENKO: Then what is the problem? You know how everyone straggles in after an opening night. [*To* GLEMOV] And you are?

GLEMOV: Gleb Glemov. I am playing Stalin.

> *A long pause.*

KLIMENKO: Creative casting. Klimenko, young Soviet hero cum romantic lead.

MOKHOVA: Comrade Glemov, you are leaving.

GLEMOV: Yes I am.

KLIMENKO: By the way, saw Babelev just now heading up to the typists. Says he's got script changes.

MOKHOVA: He can't have. Who authorised them?

KLIMENKO: I sincerely wish I could care, Comrade.

MOKHOVA: This will go in my report. [*Exiting, to* GLEMOV] Comrade, I don't expect to see you when I get back.

MOKHOVA *exits.*

GLEMOV: She won't let me sit in on the rehearsal.

KLIMENKO: Best not to mess with Comrade Mokhova. I took the piss out of her in my first show and got a dressing-room so far from the stage I needed travel papers to make my cue. [*Looking at* GLEMOV*'s shoes*] You got big feet.

GLEMOV: I suppose.

KLIMENKO: Size twelve?

GLEMOV: Elevens.

KLIMENKO: Pity. [*Pause.*] Personally, I like stage managers who hate actors. In a bullshit business, it's good that someone's not flinging it around. And also, [*lowering his voice*] you can guess where her little reports are going to, if you know what I mean.

GLEMOV: It is just that the woman below me cooks cabbage, but you see—

KLIMENKO: Is she pickling the cabbage?

GLEMOV: Um… err… I don't know. But there's an awful lot of cabbage, and anyway—

KLIMENKO: Really? Where do you think she gets the cabbage?

GLEMOV: From the Party store, I suppose. Her husband's a member.

KLIMENKO: So Party cabbage! That's good cabbage. Listen, next time you see her, tell her your friend can get hold of one litre and half-litre pickling jars.

GLEMOV: [*confused*] My friend?

KLIMENKO: Me.

GLEMOV: You know, I don't really know her.

KLIMENKO: Then get to know her. God! She's a Party Member!

GLEMOV: You mean like 'pull'?

KLIMENKO: No, not 'pull'. Where does this cynicism come from? I ask myself. No, friendship. Aren't we all comrades sharing these hard days of social reconstruction? And can any of us do it on our own? So, I make friends with you, you make friends with her. And what do we have? A community—people who care, people who share: friends.

NADEZDA IVANOVA SHILOVSKYA *(*NADIA*) enters, an old, elegant actress of the old tradition. Overdressed, she is perspiring and out of breath. She carries a handbag and a string bag with parcels in it.*

NADIA: Who's in, Klimenko?

KLIMENKO: Just us so far, Nadia. Mokhova has us all on report. [*Aside to* GLEMOV] Now, if want to talk about 'pull'… [*To* NADIA] You might be a bit overdressed, Nadia.

NADIA: Yes. Were I young, I would find myself a summer frock for days like these, but there is a dignity that age requires that tends towards the heavier types of cloth. [*Looking into a compact mirror, dabbing away the sweat*] Oh, dear! But of course, you wind up looking undignified anyway, because you sweat like a Black Sea pig. I will need to re-powder as soon as the tide has ebbed. [*She takes off her jacket.*] Is the samovar lit, do we know?

KLIMENKO: I've only just arrived myself. Now, Nadia, there's a little something that I need to chat to you about.

NADIA: Certainly. You couldn't drop my jacket off in my dressing-room, could you?

KLIMENKO: With pleasure. Maybe we could find some time—

NADIA: And a cup of tea? Add a dash of cold water to cool it down. Thank you, you are a dear.

KLIMENKO: Of course, Nadia. We will chat later?

KLIMENKO *starts to exit with the jacket.*

NADIA: Oh, I'm sure. And could you ask young Mokhova to see me, please.

MOKHOVA *enters from downstage.*

MOKHOVA: I'm here, Nadia.

NADIA: Ah, Mokhova, child, I seem to have lost my script.

MOKHOVA: No, you haven't. You left it backstage. I'll bring it to you.

NADIA: No, I shall come for it presently. I am not the Tsarina—as we used to say in the old days.

MOKHOVA: Unfortunately, it seems there have been some changes already.

But it will not disrupt the schedule. The typists have them now.

NADIA: Oh, dear, I hope that this will not be one of those plays that change with every sneeze of the censor. My old brain will not cope, I swear. [*Her string bag*] Oh, and child, I managed a little extra sugar this month, so I have been baking. Now, this larger one is for you and the crew when they come in this afternoon. You'll find a little butter in a tin—if it hasn't melted in this heat—but you must promise to keep it from the greedy actors. Especially our Ukrainian colleague, or it will find its way to the black market by lunchtime.

MOKHOVA: Thank you, Nadia. It will be appreciated.

NADIA: The smaller one is for the cast.

MOKHOVA: [*confidentially*] And is there any word?

NADIA: Word? Oh, no. No word yet.

MOKHOVA: Oh, but—

NADIA: These things take time. Don't be despondent, child. [*To* GLEMOV] And who are you?

GLEMOV: Gleb Egorovich Glemov.

MOKHOVA: Comrade Glemov is leaving.

NADIA: And what is it that you do, young man?

GLEMOV: I'm a goalkeeper.

NADIA: How delightful! Although you seem to have strayed out of your penalty box.

MOKHOVA: Comrade Glemov has been hired to play Comrade General Secretary Stalin in the play, but he is not needed until Wednesday.

GLEMOV: This is all new to me so I was hoping to sit in. See how it's done.

NADIA: Oh, young man, I must warn you that you are in grave danger. Theatre is quite the most marvellous world, utterly seductive, that once experienced may turn your head. You are a goner if you get the bug! [*Catching* MOKHOVA*'s negative expression*] Nevertheless, it seems you'll have to wait until Wednesday to be infected. Rules are rules, after all.

GLEMOV: [*preparing to leave*] Right, I suppose I will see you on Wednesday then.

NADIA: [*to* MOKHOVA] But perhaps you might want to reconsider, child. You and I are both sticklers for regulations, I know, such a bore, but it might do the young man good to watch proceedings. At the very least, he will learn that footballers are not the only ones overpraised for their meagre accomplishments.

MOKHOVA: He must go.

NADIA: Must he? Not even to indulge an old woman's whim?

MOKHOVA: Nadia...

NADIA: You would be doing me a favour...

> MOKHOVA *considers and surprisingly changes her mind.*

MOKHOVA: All right. He may stay.

NADIA: Bless you, child. A reprieve from the authorities, young man!

MOKHOVA: But only until dinner break. The commissary has not been advised and I'm not filling in extra forms.

> MOKHOVA *starts to exit.*

NADIA: Oh, and, child?

MOKHOVA: Yes?

NADIA: Remind me. Am I playing a babushka or a dowager in this one?

MOKHOVA: A babushka, ma'am.

> MOKHOVA *exits.*

NADIA: A babushka. So it's on with the motley! You know, young man, in the days of the Imperial theatres I played all manner of roles—ingénues and lovers and temptresses and good wives and grasping merchant women—but now age has reduced me to only two: either a dowager in an Ostrovsky or suchlike, or a babushka in a recent work of socialist realism, a peasant grandmamma, who speaks her simple folk wisdom to the young and restless proletariat. I must have played dozens of them by now. It's all quite a bore. Nevertheless, I do try to enliven each characterisation with something distinctive, such as a lisp or, should I feel daring, a limp.

GLEMOV: Thank you for squaring things with Mokhova. You see, the lady beneath me cooks cabbage and because—

NADIA: Oh, I once played a babushka who hoarded cabbage.

GLEMOV: Oh…

NADIA: Quite selfishly, a dreadful kulak woman during the collectivisations. My grandson, a dutiful Pioneer, 'shopped me' to the authorities, and at the play's dénouement, I was dispatched shamefaced to the gulag.

GLEMOV: Oh dear.

NADIA: Surprisingly powerful. Now, your name again, young man?

GLEMOV: Gleb Egorovich…

NADIA: Just your surname. With my incipient senility I have the devil of a time trying to keep track of patronymics.

GLEMOV: Glemov.

NADIA: Of course, thank you. Glemov. Glemov. I think the fraying net of memory has gathered it up, Glemov. And you play Stalin in our little birthday show, Glemov. Of course, I could call everyone Comrade in the new Soviet style and dispense with names altogether, but I am far too old to be taught new tricks. Does my confession shock you, Glemov? Will you 'shop me' to the authorities?

GLEMOV: [*warming to her*] Oh, I would never do that… er… Madame.

NADIA: Oh, please, not Madame. Not Madame! Dear me, do I seem that grand? No, Nadia, you must call me Nadia. Everyone does.

GLEMOV: Thank you, Nadia.

NADIA: Now we are thoroughly acquainted, Glemov, may I venture a small observation from which I hope you shall not draw offence?

GLEMOV: What's that?

NADIA: A small thing to do with your role as Stalin.

GLEMOV: Yes.

NADIA: You look nothing like him.

GLEMOV: A few people have said that.

NADIA: Yes, Glemov, but I have actually met the Great Man once or twice, seeing him at close quarters as few people have, and can personally vouch that there is not a scintilla of similarity between you. Your face carries none of his features. You are smooth, he is hairy. You are fair, he is dark. He is heavy set, you are slim. You are tall and strong, while he is—well, let us say—less tall and has other strengths. I must say that your lack of resemblance to him is uncanny.

GLEMOV: [*pulling out his pipe*] I do have a pipe.

> KAMEV *and* DINSKY *enter in their shirt sleeves, carrying their jackets and scripts.* KAMEV *(*LEON GRIGORYEVICH*) is in his early fifties;* DINSKY, *forty-ish, is something of his loyal lieutenant.*

KAMEV: No, not there, where I go, 'You youngsters are forgetting the lessons of 1917!'

DINSKY: You do that so well.

KAMEV: Yes, I think so—with modesty. But who would know? With that rag distracting everybody.

DINSKY: Your best line.

KAMEV: Well, I have got those others at the Factory Meeting. But one of my best lines, certainly. [*To* NADIA] Ah, good morning, Nadia. You are looking radiant.

NADIA: Heatstroke, I expect.

DINSKY: Yes, a very warm day.

KAMEV: Dinsky and I have been sauntering along the embankment in our shirt sleeves like two carefree bachelors.

NADIA: You are in good spirits, Kamev.

KAMEV: Opened last night in Babelev's latest opusculum, didn't we?

DINSKY: A romantic comedy of unparalleled charm and delicacy.

KAMEV: Set in a ball-bearing factory.

DINSKY: Boy meets girl.

KAMEV: Girl meets boy.

DINSKY: Boy and girl meet their production quotas.

KAMEV: A tale to rouse the heart.

DINSKY: And move one to tears.

NADIA: Now, you two, you are being perilously satirical.

KAMEV: Not at all. We had three curtain calls.

DINSKY: More like two and a half. The last was a little half-hearted.

KAMEV: Yes, but didn't we milk it well?

DINSKY: Like pros.

KAMEV: The critics will be too afraid to say it, but I think the performances flattered the rather turgid script.

DINSKY: Leon Grigoryevich was quite brilliant.

KAMEV: Was I, old friend? That's very kind of you. Despite my misfortune?

DINSKY: [*explaining*] Larissa Yakonova upstaged him.

NADIA: You poor fellow.

KAMEV: On my best line.

DINSKY: Liar! You just said one of your best.

KAMEV: Well, I've warmed to it. I was building up to my savage exposure of the Trotskyist wreckers in the assembly line and she started dabbing her face with the biggest, reddest handkerchief seen outside a bullring. Was going to say something to her afterwards—

DINSKY: 'Steady on, my girl, that's not how theatre professionals behave to one another.'

KAMEV: —but I restrained myself.

DINSKY: Kept his dignity.

NADIA: Well, one must be forgiving with actors who are still learning their craft, Kamev.

DINSKY: *Noblesse oblige*.

KAMEV: I suppose, but she only got the role because… No, I shan't.

DINSKY: The rest is silence.

KAMEV: Though—is she in this morning?—because now might be a better time to take her aside and gently point out her *faux pas*.

NADIA: I don't know, Kamev, it is never a good idea to cause discord, no matter how much one is provoked. [*To* GLEMOV] We have to work so intimately with one another, a bad atmosphere can make rehearsals hellish.

KAMEV: At any rate, I refuse to allow her want of technique to spoil our triumph. Three curtain calls. Dinsky here did a lovely bit of business with his cane.

DINSKY: You saw that?

KAMEV: An exquisite comic touch.

DINSKY: I saved it for opening, but I'm afraid it's a crib. Stole it from Charlie Chaplin, *The Gold Rush*.

KAMEV: Immaterial—everybody steals, the trick's to steal from the best, which you did magnificently.

DINSKY: [*a little bow*] *Merci, mon ami*.

KAMEV: Now, Nadezda Ivanova, this young fellow grinning cheerfully beside you has not been introduced.

DINSKY: Perhaps he is her latest lover.

KAMEV: Not another!

DINSKY: She will use you up and discard the husk, young man!

NADIA: Dinsky, please. Keep your crudities for the streets. Anyway, his name is—don't tell me—Glemov.

GLEMOV: Gleb Egorovich…

DINSKY: The Black Panther!

GLEMOV: Well, yes.

KAMEV: Do you know him, Dinsky?

DINSKY: Admired him from the football terraces. He's the goalie for the Dinamo, celebrated with the nickname 'The Black Panther'.

GLEMOV: [explaining] You see, the outfit is black.

DINSKY: And he leaps about.

KAMEV: Does he?

DINSKY: He pounces in an incredibly athletic and cat-like way.

KAMEV: A footballing Nijinsky! Hooray for you, Gleb Egorovich! [Shaking his hand] I am Kamev and this is Dinsky, whose deep love and knowledge of the sporting life I must say always surprises me.

DINSKY: Were you not a complete philistine when it comes to anything that occurs outside of theatre, Leon Grigoryevich, you would be as thrilled meeting him as I.

KAMEV: A sporting legend?

DINSKY: His feats against the Turks and the Czechs are still spoken of in awe. The city is still abuzz about his recent save against Fedotov, the Red Army striker. A real cannonball that broke his wrist.

GLEMOV: [tapping his cast] Actually, it wasn't the shot, it was the landing. Out for the rest of the season.

DINSKY: Good news for all us Spartak fans anyway!

GLEMOV: Oh, I think you'll find young Shadrev will keep your strikers at bay!

NADIA: If you gentlemen are going to discuss football, I'll take my opportunity to freshen up. I sent Klimenko off to fetch some tea, but I fear he's gone and traded it for a pair of stockings.

NADIA *moves to exit.*

KAMEV: We shall alert you when Trifinov gets in. [*Aside*] No doubt up half the night giving Yakonova her notes. But no, that is beneath me. So you're a sporting immortal then, Glemov?

GLEMOV: I suppose—while my career lasts.

KAMEV: Ah, temporarily immortal. We in the theatre know that ontology, don't we, Dinsky?

DINSKY: *Sic transit gloria.*

KAMEV: We were once stars in the provinces.

DINSKY: True, though Leon Grigoryevich was a star of a far greater magnitude.

KAMEV: No, no. While that has generally been the case according to billing, Dinsky frequently outshone me in performance.

DINSKY: Never!

KAMEV: Your Iago in Rostov, for example.

DINSKY: Ah, yes…

KAMEV: I was the noble blackamoor, but even I paled in comparison!

DINSKY: No, this is outrageous flattery and I won't have it.

KAMEV: Take it, Dinsky, it is your due. Particularly now that we are returned to Moscow and are treated like shit.

DINSKY: A tad strong.

KAMEV: No, we must call a spade a spade and shit, shit. Our reputations have counted for nothing this past year, nobody has heard of us. [*To* GLEMOV] Have you?

GLEMOV: No…

KAMEV: [*disappointed*] Really?

GLEMOV: But I don't go to the theatre very much.

KAMEV: That is no excuse. When Dinsky and I toured with *Woe from Wit* to Irkutsk in '32, crowds met the train.

DINSKY: At railway sidings, woodcutters and peasants would come out of nowhere to gawp at us.

KAMEV: We signed autographs for people who couldn't read! Because they had heard of Dinsky and Kamev and my late wife Rula Leshkova.

DINSKY: Who was a superb talent. Sadly missed.

KAMEV: [*suddenly subdued*] Yes, thank you, Dinsky. She was incomparable. And she was by my side when I played the great roles, one after the other. Trigorin and the lovesick major, and Professor Storitsyn, and Kalestikov in *The Inspector General*...

DINSKY: And Shakespeare.

KAMEV: Russia's greatest playwright—don't care where he was born, a mere detail. He had a Russian soul. Hamlet and Mercutio and Shylock. Beautiful words. What joy! To feel those words in your mouth as you release them into the black void of the auditorium is the most sensual pleasure.

DINSKY: It's very nice.

KAMEV: But now what do I play?

DINSKY: Old Lathe Operator.

KAMEV: Old Lathe Operator. The character doesn't even have a name, for Godsake! And what do I say? What honeyed phrases seep from his wise old lips? [*Switching to a working-class accent*] 'Comrade, that sort of defeatist talk will not get Central Committee Resolution 514 finished on time!'

DINSKY: He says it well, though.

KAMEV: How can an artist who has spoken the finest music created for the human voice be expected to chew on such cardboard?

DINSKY: Just as bad for me. I play Committee Man.

KAMEV: And to add insult to the gravest injury...

DINSKY: Ah, yes.

KAMEV: ... I had to audition! It was humiliating.

      KLIMENKO *enters with a cup of tea on a saucer.*

KLIMENKO: Morning all. Nadia? Anyone seen her?

KAMEV: Klimenko, please, you're interrupting a story.

GLEMOV: To the dressing-rooms, I think.

KLIMENKO: Oh, Comrade Jesus Christ! I was just there.

KAMEV: Well, that's where she went. Now, if you please.

KLIMENKO: Sure. Feet, what size, Dinsky?

DINSKY: Nine.

KLIMENKO: Sorry.

DINSKY: Oh, bugger!

> KLIMENKO *exits with the tea.*

KAMEV: [*continuing*] It was infuriating—

> KLIMENKO *returns.*

KLIMENKO: [*to* DINSKY] Got your razor blades, though.

> KLIMENKO *throws a small packet which* DINSKY *catches with glee.*

DINSKY: Excellent! Bravo! Fix you up later, then?

KLIMENKO: Sure. Carry on.

> KLIMENKO *exits with the tea.*

DINSKY: He's a lifesaver, that Klimenko. I've been on my last blade for three weeks. [*To* GLEMOV] Look at those cuts.

KAMEV: Am I permitted to continue?

DINSKY: Sorry. I'll give you your cue, shall I? [*With dramatic emphasis*] Glemov, even I was shocked when Leon Grigoryevich had to audition.

KAMEV: It was infuriating. I haven't auditioned since I was a juvenile in repertory. It boggles the reason. I mean, does thirty-five years in this profession count for nothing? Does Hamlet and Ivan the Terrible count for nothing? In the meantime, upstarts, suck-ups and party lackeys are walking off the street and into plum roles. There was a time when talent was the only criterion in casting, but now— [*Realising he may be criticising the system, he covers.*] Granted, we live in the perfect democratic society and all things in all ways are immeasurably better than the old days, and so on and so forth—but that aside, it gives me the screaming pip!

DINSKY: Yes, but remember, Leon Grigoryevich, there are no small roles, only small actors.

KAMEV: But that is exactly my point, Dinsky. The small roles should go to the small actors. That's what small actors are for! I have no business playing a nameless lathe operator. I have—modestly—vast talents going to waste, tremendous emotional reserves just sitting idle.

DINSKY: Rather *infra dig.*

KAMEV: Isn't it supposed to be 'each according to their capacities' or
    something or other—didn't I see that on a poster somewhere?

DINSKY: I'm a bit rusty on the slogan side of things…

GLEMOV: 'Egalitarianism is not socialism'—that's one.

KAMEV: [*now very worked up*] That'll do! Egalitarianism is not socialism.
    Which means—does it not?—that we are not equally endowed in
    our gifts and cannot be equally treated. Yes, it makes no more sense
    my playing Old Lathe Operator as, say, putting Dinsky in goal for
    Moscow Dinamo, or giving you the lead role in a play. There is a
    natural aristocracy of talent—

DINSKY: And you would be our Tsar, Leon Grigoryevich!

KAMEV: Would I—? [*Beat. Changing, shaking his head*] Ah, Dinsky!
    You've caught me again. Dinsky! I hang my head in shame. The
    actor's ego! My fatal, fatal flaw! [*To* GLEMOV] You see, Glemov,
    everyone should have a comrade—and I mean that in the old-
    fashioned sense—a comrade like Dinsky, a leveller. Someone to
    keep your feet planted on solid earth.

DINSKY: I just like to remind him that we are all servants to the art.

KAMEV: Yes, but why can't some other servant empty the chamber pot?

> DIMITRI BABELEV, *the playwright, enters, thirties, a bundle of
> nervous energy.*

BABELEV: Where's Trifinov?

DINSKY: [*clapping*] Bravo! Author!

BABELEV: Yeah, yeah, yeah. Where is he?

DINSKY: Not in yet.

BABELEV: It's twenty past, for Pete's sake!

DINSKY: Perhaps he is in a bread queue.

KAMEV: Four curtain calls last night, Babelev. Big night for you.

BABELEV: Did you get a look into the box?

KAMEV: I was acting.

BABELEV: You couldn't look up a second?

DINSKY: The audience loved it.

BABELEV: Who gives a shit about the audience? Did the Artistic Affairs
    guys like it?

KAMEV: You can't see the box. You can't see past the first two rows. I heard Trifinov went in search of them.

BABELEV: When?

KAMEV: Afterwards, but I don't think he caught them. Where were you?

BABELEV: They left straightaway? Oh shit.

DINSKY: Is that bad?

BABELEV: Of course it's bad. [*Beat.*] Or it could be good. [*Beat.*] What it is is uncertain. And that's bad.

DINSKY: It was a Friday night. Maybe they just rushed home to their families.

BABELEV: Yeah, and maybe they rushed home to write their denunciations for Pravda.

KAMEV: [*with an accent*] 'Comrade, that sort of defeatist talk will not get Resolution 514 finished on time.'

BABELEV: [*blankly*] What are you talking about?

KAMEV: Don't you recognise your own sterling prose? It is from your play *Precision Milled* that opened to rapturous applause last night. My young friend, you are in a state. Take advice from an old stager: enjoy your success, it will be fleeting enough. In this business you are only as good as your latest show.

DINSKY: And your latest show is a triumph.

BABELEV: Yeah, yeah, yeah, you're right. How many curtain calls?

KAMEV: Four or five.

DINSKY: At least.

KAMEV: They stood and cheered, Babelev. That's got to count for something. They can't ignore that.

BABELEV: Oh, yes they can. What about that Shostakovich opera? Standing ovations, great reviews, full houses, the lot. Then what happened? Somebody—and we all know who—didn't like it and, bang, *Pravda* slammed it. Overnight, this great opera has gone from hit to shit. It is bourgeois and formalist and riddled with the dread 'M word'.

KAMEV: Well, if it was riddled with the 'M word'…

BABELEV: And where is the great Shostakovich now?

DINSKY: Isn't he writing film scores?

BABELEV: Movies? Really. I thought he had been—you know…

DINSKY: Oh, no I don't think so. That's not what I heard.

BABELEV: He knows what he's doing. Fewer restrictions in movies. You make a political mistake and it gets edited out. Nobody need know. I've been thinking maybe switching myself. I reckon I could write a nice, breezy comedy set on a collective. Lots of songs and girls. Frolicking at harvest time. A bit of comic business with a pig. This theatre writing—I thought it would be less risky than poetry, but Socialist Realism is a killer.

KAMEV: But you do it so well, Babelev.

BABELEV: It's the uplift, the bloody uplift. The optimism is relentless. Joy in work and hope for the future. Hope, always hope! You can't let it flag. I've put a sign over my desk to remind me, in big letters and exclamation marks—'ALWAYS UPLIFT!' God, it's depressing!

DINSKY: But it seems to be working, Babelev, your plays are full of uplift. A critic would need to be off his head to fling the dread 'M word' at you.

BABELEV: Yeah?

KAMEV: I think it can be safely said that your plays possess a Soviet purity.

DINSKY: Completely untainted by innovation and experiment.

BABELEV: You think so? It takes only one false step. With this 'M' business last month, the last thing I want is to attract the wrong type of interest.

KAMEV: Babelev, if you are worried about writing about Stalin, remember we have over four months of rehearsals, more than enough time to make certain that there is nothing interesting in the play.

BABELEV: Oh, it is already wrong. The entire project has taken a sharp detour up shit creek.

KAMEV: Now, now, Babelev.

BABELEV: No, this is serious. Last night at second interval, I bump into that jumped-up actor Moskvin. He's got hold of a draft script from somewhere. 'Oh, Babelev, old comrade, absolutely loved *Man of*

Steel, but don't you think making Marshal Yegorov a lead character a little risky?' I say, 'What do you mean? He's one of Stalin's war buddies.' He says, 'Arrested in the purge of the army—didn't you hear? Apparently ran a Trotskyist cell in Riga.' I say, 'I did all the research. He was not a Trotskyist.' 'Well,' he says, 'he'd never been to Riga either, I expect, but that didn't stop the Chekists from arresting him.'

KAMEV: That's my character.

BABELEV: So—didn't wait for the end of the show—rushed over to the Writers' Union, they have the new big *Soviet Encyclopaedia*. Look up Yegorov—entry's gone.

KAMEV: My character is gone?

BABELEV: Poof! I'm in a sweat now. Flip to the picture of Stalin with his Civil War buddies. The old encyclopaedia has Stalin and Voroshilov and between them our friend Yegorov. The new encyclopaedia shows Stalin and Voroshilov and between them—a tree stump!

KAMEV: My character is a tree stump!

BABELEV: But I worked out a solution. Some of the early lines I can off-load to other characters.

KAMEV: You're cutting my part?

BABELEV: Unless you want to play a tree stump.

KAMEV: This is unspeakable.

BABELEV: Oh, calm down, Kamev, for Pete's sake. Just cut a few lines early on to make the part less conspicuous. Dinsky gets most of them.

DINSKY: [*containing his delight*] Oh!

BABELEV: But you keep the rest, including your big speech at the end. We just change the name of your character.

KAMEV: To what?

BABELEV: Red Army Commander Two.

KAMEV: Red Army Commander Two! What sort of character name is that?

BABELEV: A safe one.

KAMEV: Red Army Commander Two!

BABELEV: Well, I can't call him Yegorov, can I? Because Yegorov is not to be mentioned, and I can't disguise him with another name.

KAMEV: Why not?

BABELEV: Because that would be historically inaccurate.

KAMEV: But Red Army Commander Two—I sound like the second volume of a cheap novel.

BABELEV: Tell you what, old pal, as a favour to you, I'll keep Yegorov in the show, and you can play him, and—what do you say?—after the show opens you and I will take a long trip together in a cattle truck on the Siberian railway!

KAMEV: There is no need for sarcasm.

BABELEV: Well, what do you want me to do, for Pete's sake? Creating art is hard enough without the Cheka snatching your lead characters. I've been up all night and I'm in no mood for your actor's bullshit. So if you have a complaint about the show, take it upstairs or moan to Trifinov. And where is he, for Pete's sake?

DINSKY: Well, Yakonova isn't in yet either.

BABELEV: What? Are those two an item?

DINSKY: Oh, a mere backstage whisper. She was given extra rehearsals.

BABELEV: Oh?

DINSKY: Unscheduled—and they say the last actress Trifinov gave unscheduled rehearsals to became Trifinova. A few days ago at the loading doors, they were heard heatedly discussing the said wife.

BABELEV: Well, I don't fancy his chances of getting a divorce.

DINSKY: You got a divorce, didn't you?

BABELEV: Yeah, yeah, but that was a few years ago. Much easier then. They've tightened up, back to family values and all that crap.

KAMEV: I thought you lived with your wife.

BABELEV: I do. I hate the bitch but I can't move out. Where am I going to get another apartment? It's absolute hell, five years of it. She sleeps with the kid and I sleep on a cot in the kitchen.

KAMEV: [*astonished*] You have a kitchen?

BABELEV: Kitchenette, but it's practically separate. Writers' Union accommodation. The flat's an absolute monster—thirty-six square

metres, plus kitchenette, plus a corner alcove with a window where
I have my desk, running water, good steam heating and a bathroom
shared with only two other families.

DINSKY *gives a low whistle.*

Yeah, and I'm supposed to give that up and let some housing committee
shove me into a bachelor cubicle with a bunch of unwashed factory
hands—bugger off! I'd rather live with my fucked-up ex-wife and
my whiney kid.

DINSKY: That's tough.

BABELEV: Yeah, yeah, and it's going to get worse if she remarries. So if
Trifinov wants a divorce, he better be prepared to have his honeymoon
in a broom cupboard.

KAMEV: And did you see the piece of business she added last night?

BABELEV: Yakonova? Oh, yeah, second act with the red hankie?

KAMEV: More like the Soviet flag!

BABELEV: No doubt about it, the girl's got talent. It is just what that scene
needs. But, Kamev, you have got to give it a bit more air.

KAMEV: More air?

BABELEV: You're speaking right over it, pulling the focus.

KAMEV: But she's upstaging me!

BABELEV: Believe me, Kamev, no-one could upstage you.

KAMEV: Unbelievable!

BABELEV: By the way, Dinsky, loved the business with the cane. A truly
original touch.

DINSKY: Well, thank you, sir.

KAMEV: [*mostly to himself*] Outrageous! The way I get treated is just
outrageous.

BABELEV: [*to* GLEMOV] Hey, I didn't think you were in today?

GLEMOV: Well, you see, the lady below me cooks cabbage—

BABELEV: Hey, if you're here we can go through the new changes. See
if they work.

KAMEV: What's going on? He's a goalkeeper.

BABELEV: Didn't you know? He's playing Stalin.

KAMEV *is gobsmacked.*

DINSKY: Oh, congratulations! Our Man of Steel!

KAMEV: He's playing Stalin?

BABELEV: Yeah, yeah. Trifinov found him.

KAMEV: But it's the lead character.

BABELEV: No, he's the title character, there's a difference. He has fewer lines than almost anybody.

KAMEV: Yes, but the character has a name!

BABELEV: Oh God, Kamev!

KAMEV: He is a goalkeeper! He has no experience.

GLEMOV: Um, I once played a shepherd in a nativity play.

BABELEV: There, see? Experience. Though, Glemov, best keep that to yourself—sounds a bit counter-revolutionary.

GLEMOV: I was only seven.

BABELEV: Even so.

KAMEV: This is insufferable. The last straw. I'm taking this upstairs.

> KAMEV *exits upstage. He almost collides with* KLIMENKO, *still carrying a cup of tea.*

KLIMENKO: Hey, watch out! Has she been here?

BABELEV: Who?

KLIMENKO: Nadia. I've got her tea here.

GLEMOV: She's not been back.

KLIMENKO: Babelev, size shoes?

BABELEV: [*hopefully*] Ten and a half.

KLIMENKO: Sorry.

BABELEV: I can squeeze into a ten.

KLIMENKO: Nope, but I might have a lead on your typewriter ribbon. Give me two days. Where could she disappear to? This is not the Bolshoi.

> KLIMENKO *exits.*

BABELEV: You can say that again. The director turns up on time at the Bolshoi. [*Exiting*] Look, I'm seeing Mokhova. As soon as the typists have finished the scripts, we'll run through the changes, Trifinov or no Trifinov. At least we can get something done this morning.

> BABELEV *exits.*

DINSKY: The atmosphere is always tense after an opening night, waiting for the reviews to come in. The critics in this town can be murder.

GLEMOV: This is all very strange to me.

DINSKY: Strange and sort of wonderful, I expect.

GLEMOV: Mainly strange, I think. Everybody talks so much. A lot of it is just going over my head.

DINSKY: Well, I'm sure we have our jargon, as I'm sure you have in football, which seems perfectly natural to you, but leaves outsiders scratching their heads. Like, you know, 'offside trap' or 'the long ball'.

GLEMOV: Yeah, I get it. Like—the 'M word'?

DINSKY: See, I have no idea. Is it manager? M for manager… or midfield something-or-other… No, give up, what?

GLEMOV: I don't know.

DINSKY: Right. Maybe you can ask your coach.

GLEMOV: No, it's in theatre, the 'M word'. You were just talking about it just then. The 'dread M word'. Shostakovich was called it.

DINSKY: [*dawning, loudly*] Oh, Meyerholdism! [*Whispering*] Shhhh, sorry, it isn't something one shouts out loud in a theatre.

GLEMOV: So, what is it?

DINSKY: Meyerholdism? Well, it's hard to say really, to be honest, no-one really knows. But it's best to avoid it if you can. Especially since… you know.

GLEMOV: Sorry…

DINSKY: [*looking around, lowering his voice*] He was snatched.

GLEMOV: Who?

DINSKY: Meyerhold, the chap who invented Meyerholdism.

GLEMOV: Have I heard of him?

DINSKY: I should expect so. Biggest thing in theatre, or was. Once there were only two directors whose names people in the street recognised. The first was Stanislavski…

GLEMOV: Oh, yeah, I know him.

DINSKY: Yes, ran the Moscow Art Theatre, old chap, died just last year. And the other chappie was Meyerhold, who was snatched last month in Leningrad, so, you see, the theatre is a little short of geniuses at the moment.

GLEMOV: What did he do wrong?

DINSKY: Meyerhold? Don't know. Can't say. Who knows? I'm sure they had their reasons. They have been unhappy with him for some time, so no-one was surprised when... Apparently, the warrant was signed by the new NKVD boss what's-his-face.

GLEMOV: Beria.

DINSKY: Beria. That's the chap. So poor old M's in hot water and no mistake. So, for the last month we theatre folk have been keeping our heads down. Not a peep of protest when they snatched him, except for his wife, who's been trying to get us to kick up a fuss. But nobody wants to know. We see her coming with her petition and we look the other way and hope she hasn't spotted us. I wish she'd stop it. I mean, we feel sorry for her, but she puts us in a very awkward position. Sorry, you don't know who I'm talking about, do you?

GLEMOV: Um, no...

DINSKY: Zinaida Raikh.

GLEMOV: She's an actress, right?

DINSKY: Big actress. Zinaida Raikh. Starred in most of Meyerhold's shows, all the plum roles. Which is half her problem. Some think he favoured her too much, considering her range. Anyway, that caused a lot of bad blood over the years, women not getting the parts they thought they deserved. You know women and all that. So, their sympathy is tainted with an eensy bit of *schadenfreude*. When they see Zina coming along and they cross the street, some can't help skipping.

> KLIMENKO *enters, still with the cup of tea.*

KLIMENKO: Look, I'm just going to stand here and the old dear can come to me. Zina who?

GLEMOV: Raikh.

KLIMENKO: [*alarmed*] She's not in here with her useless petition, is she?

DINSKY: Oh, no. I was just getting our new boy up to exam level, that's all. [*To* GLEMOV] It's the new theatrical hoodoo. It was once forbidden to mention Macbeth in a theatre, now it's the Meyerholds. Oh, bugger me! I just said Macbeth, didn't I? Blast! I just said it again! Excuse me!

DINSKY *rushes out.*

KLIMENKO: I might as well chuck this, it's gone cold now.

GLEMOV: Where's he gone?

KLIMENKO: [*placing the cup of tea on the table*] Who knows? Probably the alley to perform some bullshit bourgeois superstition. These provincial actors are full of them. You'd do well to forget about Meyerhold.

GLEMOV: Sure. I just asked him what Meyerholdism was.

KLIMENKO: And what did he tell you?

GLEMOV: He didn't really say.

KLIMENKO: Well, I can say: it's bullshit.

GLEMOV: Right. We talked about Stanislavski too.

KLIMENKO: More bullshit.

GLEMOV: Right.

KLIMENKO: All that theory's bullshit. Take my word for it. I mean, what did Russian theatre ever do to deserve two great thinkers like Stanislavski and Meyerhold? One guy says everything on stage has to be real, the other says, no, everything has to be fake. And then they proceed to argue this point for forty bloody years! And their followers were worse. I worked with an actress a few seasons back who'd spent just five weeks or something at the Art Theatre with Stanislavski. Completely infected. She kept this fat chunk of wood in her pocket that she'd sniff before she went on stage. Poplar wood. She said it helped her to imagine the country estate—you know, the breeze wafting through the poplar trees. I thought, oh Comrade H Christ! You're only playing the maid, sweetheart. Just walk on, pick up the old girl's bags and get off.

GLEMOV: So Meyerhold was better.

KLIMENKO: No, he was just as flaky. His thing was exercises.

GLEMOV: Like weight training?

KLIMENKO: Oh, God, no. Body awareness exercises. Biomechanics, he
called it. Which is the sort of name they went crazy about in the
twenties. The first part sounds like science, the second part sounds
like engineering. The old Bolsheviks went 'Ooh, biomechanics!
That sounds good, Meyerhold!'

GLEMOV: Was it good?

KLIMENKO: No. It was just pantomime and circus bullshit. I picked
up a bit of it coming through. Jumping on another guy's chest, or
three guys becoming a horse and rider. There was one really weird
exercise—'Stabbing with the Dagger'. It was just bullshit stuff you
had to learn at theatre school. Nobody uses it in performance, well not
anymore. Not since they closed the Meyerhold.

GLEMOV: So no use to someone like me?

KLIMENKO: Don't waste your time.

GLEMOV: It is just that my acting coach says I need to loosen up.

KLIMENKO: [*sensing an opportunity*] Well, I don't know, it is useful for
warm-ups, I suppose.

GLEMOV: She said I moved as if I had borrowed someone else's body.

KLIMENKO: Yeah, now you mention it, I do detect a little muscular
rigidity. Maybe this stuff never did much for me because, you know,
I get on stage and I'm at home. I relax. It's a gift. But who knows?—
a few mime exercises might help. Someone acquainted with this
biomechanical stuff might be able to give you a few tips.

GLEMOV: You? Could you give, perhaps…?

KLIMENKO: Well, I could, I suppose, but…

GLEMOV: I'd pay you.

KLIMENKO: Oh, I wouldn't take your money.

GLEMOV: Oh…

KLIMENKO: But… say, a couple of match tickets?

GLEMOV: Oh, easy—for next Saturday?

KLIMENKO: Sure. In the stands would be good.

GLEMOV: I can put you on the halfway line.

KLIMENKO: Well, that's very generous of you. You see how our friendship
is beginning to pay dividends. All right. Lesson one. Let me see. Let's
start with something you know.

GLEMOV: Sure.

KLIMENKO: A little biomechanical exercise we'll call: 'Saving the Shot'.

GLEMOV: Oh, yeah, I got you.

KLIMENKO: I'm the centre forward, you're the goalie. I'll mime shooting, you mime saving. Go over there and pretend you're in goal. But we'll have to listen out for people coming—this Meyerhold stuff is contraband, if you know what I mean.

GLEMOV: I guess.

KLIMENKO: Now, I have a ball.

> *He holds up an imaginary ball and drops it at his feet and, to his commentary, dribbles past two defenders and shoots.*

Are you ready? Klimenko has the ball for Kiev, he passes the halfback, he passes the fullback, just the goalie to beat, he looks up, he shoots!

> GLEMOV *'saves' the shot by taking the imaginary ball high.* DINSKY *enters from the rear of the stage and watches.*

GLEMOV: And Glemov saves!

KLIMENKO: No, he didn't. I hit it to your other side. It's a goal!

GLEMOV: Oh, bugger!

> *As* GLEMOV *retrieves the 'ball' from the back of the 'net' and rolls it back to* KLIMENKO...

KLIMENKO: You see, you weren't imagining the same ball as me. That's the first lesson in biomechanics, always pay attention to what the other guy is doing.

> DINSKY *moves down.*

DINSKY: What are you doing?

KLIMENKO: Nothing. I'm just instructing our friend in a few tricks of the trade.

DINSKY: That's not biomechanics.

KLIMENKO: As if you would know.

DINSKY: I'll show you. Give me the ball, please.

KLIMENKO: [*picking up the 'ball' and holding it away*] No, I'm teaching him.

DINSKY: Please. He needs to know how to do these things properly.

KLIMENKO: What do you know about it?

DINSKY: [*trying to wrestle it from him*] More than you'd think. More than you, Sunny Jim. Come on. Give it up.

GLEMOV: Comrades.

DINSKY: Give it to me.

> KLIMENKO *holds the 'ball' away and above his head where* DINSKY *'jumping' cannot reach it.*

KLIMENKO: No, no. It's my ball.

> *They wrestle some more.*

Tell you what, if you want the ball so much…

> KLIMENKO *makes a break and kicks the ball into the auditorium.* DINSKY *watches it disappear into the distance.*

… you can go and get it.

DINSKY: That was a rotten thing to do, Klimenko.

GLEMOV: [*heading into the auditorium*] I'll get it!

DINSKY: [*turning*] No, Glemov, come back, don't be silly. It went into the dress circle. And we don't need it. It wasn't a proper biomechanical exercise in any case. We'll do something else.

KLIMENKO: You don't know what you're talking about.

DINSKY: I know biomechanics. [*To* GLEMOV] I'll teach you a classic exercise called 'Shooting the Bow'.

KLIMENKO: Don't pay any attention, Glemov. He knows nothing.

GLEMOV: It doesn't matter, Comrades. Really.

DINSKY: Now, watch me. Move upstage so you have a better view.

KLIMENKO: He's spent his whole career in bench-seat theatres playing Gogol to goat herders.

DINSKY: There is a little story attached to this one.

KLIMENKO: Where did you pick this up from? Some old actor in Kazakhstan?

DINSKY: You are in a forest…

KLIMENKO: Omsk?

DINSKY: [*snapping*] Meyerhold. Meyerhold taught me. Taught me himself in '22.

KLIMENKO: [*stunned*] Bullshit.

DINSKY: His first intake of students to the workshops. Ilinsky was there. Garin, Babanova, Zinaida Raikh—before he married her—Serge Eisenstein—the great film director—and I was there. Oh, yes, exalted company and Meyerhold taught us. I was there when he first worked through the études, including 'Shooting the Bow', [*turning to* GLEMOV] which I am going to show you now.

KLIMENKO: [*believing him*] I don't believe you.

DINSKY: So, you are a hunter running through the forest. You see your quarry, stop, take an arrow from your quiver, place it on the bowstring, pull back, shoot and strike. Now, this is biomechanics, it is not mime. So, it may seem a little strange. But anyway, it goes…

> DINSKY *carries out the biomechanical étude. And, indeed, it is very strange. It begins and ends in a 'dactyl', and consists of a furious crouched run in a circle, a stop, pulling the arrow from the quiver, drawing the bow, shooting, a clap, and a shout 'Ha!', and another run in a circle.*

[*Finishing*] What do you think?

GLEMOV: That was…

KLIMENKO: … bloody weird.

DINSKY: Well, bit rusty…

GLEMOV: I'm not sure that's going to help me.

DINSKY: Oh, it will, believe me. It's training, like in football, you know, exercises and drills prepare you for the game. They aren't necessarily used in the game, though they can be. It breaks down the actor's movements into its various bits, you see? Every action begins and ends with a stance. So pulling back the bowstring… [*He demonstrates each component of the simple action pulling back the bowstring.*] You have a stance. Then a preparation to move which includes the resistance of the bow. A movement. A preparation to stop. A stop and *voilà*, a new stance. And in one fluid movement it goes something like this.

> *He demonstrates the entire sequence.*

GLEMOV: Sure, I see.

KLIMENKO: You know, if that Bolshevik of a stage manager waltzes in here…

DINSKY: Yes, yes, you're right, we'll cut it short for now, but I just want to give you the flavour of it. It is the most wonderful training. The things that Meyerhold taught me in those two years in the workshops I've used my entire career.

KLIMENKO: And made him one of the great actors of his generation.

DINSKY: Klimenko, why don't you go upstage and listen for anyone coming?

KLIMENKO: Whatever you say, Dinsky. But, Glemov, you're wasting your time.

DINSKY: [*to* GLEMOV] Even in the most naturalistic productions it's invaluable. [*Indicating the teacup* KLIMENKO *placed on the table*] See that cup?

GLEMOV: Yes

DINSKY: It's poisoned. The audience knows it's poisoned. They saw the villain put the poison in there. But your character is completely unaware. Now, according to Naturalism, how do you drink from the cup? What would Stanislavski tell you to do? [*He demonstrates, picking up the cup and drinking from it casually as he speaks.*] Well, drink from the cup as you would in real life, as if you didn't know it was poisoned. Well, where's the drama in that, I ask you? But old Meyerhold taught us that our job was always to be creating something for the audience. There's a cup, he'd say, and it is filled to the brim with…?

GLEMOV: Poison?

DINSKY: Significance! It carries your death in it. Your death! The audience knows if you drink from it you will die. And yet they want you to drink from the cup, because the story demands it. [*He demonstrates as he speaks, breaking down the action.*] They dread it, but they want it. So you give it to them. Nice and slow. Chop it up into smaller actions like meat for little children and they will snaffle it up. [*He lifts the cup towards his lips but, as if distracted, stops.*] And if you get it right—the rhythm, the timing, the little resistances, the tension, the clarity—the audience—I swear, [*suddenly draining the cup in a single unambiguous action*] will gasp!

KLIMENKO: Glemov, he's teaching you how to cook ham.

DINSKY: You know that bit of business with my cane last night? It was nothing, a mere bagatelle, and I pinched it from Chaplin, true, but the execution was sheer Meyerhold.

GLEMOV: So you can teach me this Meyerhold stuff?

DINSKY: Well… gosh, that's a tough one.

KLIMENKO: It certainly is, Dinsky. Because where are you going to hold your biomechanics class? Here, with denouncers hiding behind every piece of scenery.

DINSKY: [*to* GLEMOV] Yes, yes, I'm afraid he's right. These things are from another time, a lost time. So…

KLIMENKO: Someone's coming. Look, Glemov, you don't need bullshit acting theories and exercises. You're not making a career of it. Come in early on Wednesday and I will give you a few pointers to get you through.

GLEMOV: Right, okay. That's good of you.

KLIMENKO: Well, I'm a sweetheart, but don't forget the tickets.

> BABELEV *and* MOKHOVA *enter, arguing.* MOKHOVA *is holding a crisscrossed pile of replacement pages.*

BABELEV: But we are wasting time otherwise.

MOKHOVA: Comrade, I repeat, I do not have authorisation.

BABELEV: But I'm the playwright.

DINSKY: Any word on our errant director?

MOKHOVA: [*ignoring* BABELEV, *who is clearly annoying her*] I've sent the boy to his flat. But I have replacement pages here.

DINSKY: I'll take Kamev's, too.

> *Distracted,* MOKHOVA *hands* DINSKY *about twenty replacement pages. During the following, she hands out pages and the actors replace them in their scripts.*

BABELEV: We have Stalin here, keen and ready to go.

MOKHOVA: [*to* KLIMENKO *and* GLEMOV] Comrades, your new pages. [*To* BABELEV] It is not on the schedule, we cannot do it. Simple as that. Where's Kamev?

DINSKY: Ah, he sort of bobbed upstairs.

MOKHOVA: He's been told not to bother management with his complaints. If he is not back soon he goes in my report.

BABELEV: What's the point reporting him when he'll just be sitting around waiting until Trifinov turns up?

MOKHOVA: Because there are schedules, Comrade.

BABELEV: I think the Theatre Committee might want to know why you have stopped production.

MOKHOVA: I have not stopped production.

BABELEV: Well, a factory doesn't close down merely because the foreman is off sick or has overslept. Unless, of course…

Silence. Tension. Everyone replaces their pages, listening intently.

MOKHOVA: Unless what, Comrade?

BABELEV: This is a play to commemorate our leader's sixtieth birthday, a man who has lead this country successfully through these days of momentous change, and, although most people of good will are anticipating the event with joy in their hearts—

MOKHOVA: Make your point, Babelev. You are sounding like your own dialogue.

BABELEV: Maybe it will serve some elements to see this play fail.

MOKHOVA: Are you doubting my loyalty, Comrade?

BABELEV: Loyalty is easily declared, the test is in actions. Now I cannot say whether closing down rehearsals—

MOKHOVA: I'm not—

BABELEV: —or holding up rehearsals is disloyal, but it sounds to me a clear matter for Committee discussion.

MOKHOVA: [*to the others, clapping her hands*] Place your old pages in a separate pile. We don't want to mix them up.

NADIA *enters with a script and a cup of tea.*

NADIA: Isn't Trifinov in yet?

DINSKY: Overslept, I expect. Mokhova's sent Mischa to knock on his door.

MOKHOVA: I have some replacement pages for you, Nadia, but if you like I can put them in your script myself.

KLIMENKO: I can do it.

NADIA: Would you, Klimenko? You are so kind.

KLIMENKO: [*taking up the cup and saucer*] And I have your tea.

NADIA: Oh, dear. But I have a cup. I didn't know where you went, so I made my own.

KLIMENKO: I looked high and low for you.

MOKHOVA: [*passing Nadia's pages to* KLIMENKO] Here they are.

NADIA: [*to* KLIMENKO] How strange. I am a little old woman, where could I have gone?

KLIMENKO: That's exactly what I said.

NADIA: After all, this is not the Bolshoi.

KLIMENKO: That's what I said too, didn't I, Dinsky?

DINSKY: Yes, he did. Those exact words.

NADIA: How odd! You have developed a psychical ability to predict my thoughts, but not, apparently, my movements.

MOKHOVA: [*clapping*] Now if everyone could put the new pages in now, we will go through scenes seven and twelve while we're waiting for Trifinov.

NADIA: Is that a change of schedule, child?

MOKHOVA: [*hating to say it*] Yes, it is, Nadia. I'm sorry, but I assure you we will revert to the original schedule when the director arrives.

BABELEV: [*pleased he has had his way*] They're the big scenes with Stalin in them. We should make use of Glemov while he's here. If you come across any mention of General Yegorov, point it out.

KAMEV *enters with three sheets of paper, greatly agitated.*

KAMEV: A complaint form! Ten minutes waiting and then that stupid, stupid girl just hands me a complaint form—well, three complaint forms because two copies have to go to Central Office. 'Vladimir Pavelivich cannot see you now but he encourages you to place your criticisms officially in writing.' Sassy little…

DINSKY: I have your replacement pages, Kamev.

KAMEV: [*taking them, distractedly*] They know I'm not going to fill out so much paperwork. The bureaucracy is out of control.

NADIA: It was much worse in the Imperial days.

KAMEV: Well, yes, yes, of course, [*the slogan on the wall*] life is more cheerful, we know that. But what about the basic human need to get things off one's chest. I go in there. I rave for five minutes. They nod their heads. They put on their sympathetic faces. 'Oh, dear, Kamev! We'll see what we can do.' I say thank you. They close the door behind me and everybody can forget about it. I mean, I don't mind being patronised, but how dare they try to process me!

DINSKY: We all need catharsis.

MOKHOVA: [*clapping her hands*] Substitute your pages, Comrade.

KAMEV: Exactly, if they only allowed me to rant and rave, I'd stop.

BABELEV: Well, we're letting you rant and rave, but you show no sign of stopping.

KAMEV: Considering your histrionics not long ago, I find that… But, I am done, Babelev, I am done. For now, I am done.

MOKHOVA: Well, on behalf of the entire Company, I thank you, Comrade. We're going through the new scene seven—page twenty-seven B.

KAMEV: Now, which are the replacement pages?

DINSKY: The ones in your hand.

KAMEV: See! My nerves are shot.

NADIA: Am I in this one?

KLIMENKO: [*handing over her completed script*] Yes, Nadia, scene seven, there you go.

NADIA: I've had a sudden inspiration: bow legs! I think she had rickets as a child.

BABELEV: We are just reading it.

KAMEV: [*to get back at* BABELEV] You know, I think we should mark it out a little. It's too stuffy to be sitting around a table. Dinsky?

DINSKY: Oh, you know me, always happier on my feet.

BABELEV: No, I think we should just sit and read it.

MOKHOVA: [*pointedly to* BABELEV] I have no trouble with everyone marking it out, Comrade Babelev.

During the following, MOKHOVA *sets up her lectern and chair downstage and prepares. The actors also prepare, flipping through their scripts, looking for their entrances and their lines, marking certain things with pencils, etcetera. Except* GLEMOV, *who looks all at sea.*

KAMEV: Up for a stroll, Nadia?

NADIA: Oh, yes, test these bow legs. See if they go.

KLIMENKO: You enter with me, Nadia. And if you like we could have a little chat while we wait our cue…

NADIA: A little chat?

KLIMENKO: Yes, on that little matter I mentioned before, remember?

NADIA: [*tying a scarf over her hair*] I certainly remember, but we are in rehearsal, let us rehearse. Now I have a full page to wait, if you wouldn't mind fetching me a chair.

KLIMENKO: [*fetching a chair*] Not at all. Lunch break, then?

NADIA: Yes, yes, I suppose so.

GLEMOV: Sorry, what are we doing?

DINSKY: We are just walking through the scene, working out the movements.

BABELEV: None of this will be set, you know. Trifinov is only going to change it.

MOKHOVA: [*to* BABELEV] Could you read Yakonova's part, Comrade?

BABELEV: I would prefer—

MOKHOVA: There is no-one else and we wouldn't want production to stop for the want of an actor, would we? You enter with the Old Woman and Vlodya.

Everyone is ready.

Top of twenty-seven, everyone.

She reads. Note: all Man of Steel *text is in* **bold type***.*

Man of Steel. Scene seven. August 1920. A cottage near Lvov in eastern Poland, commandeered by the Red Army. Before the dawn. A Red Army Commander stands by the window.

DINSKY: [*upstage, waving at an imaginary space*] We'll have the window here, shall we? And can I have a mug of coffee?

MOKHOVA: Babelev?

BABELEV: What for?

DINSKY: It's morning. The two commanders have been on watch for hours. He needs to be alert for Stalin's return. So what about a little caffeine for verity?

BABELEV: All right. Yeah, yeah, yeah, let's get on with it.

MOKHOVA: [*adding to her prompt book*] **... stands by the window holding a mug of coffee.**

DINSKY: I'll mime it for now.

MOKHOVA: **At the table, pouring over a map of the battlefront, is Red Army Commander Two.**

KAMEV: [*under his breath*] Red Army Commander Two!

> KAMEV *pours over the 'map' while* DINSKY *gazes through the 'window' warming his hands on the 'coffee mug', taking a sip now and then, sniffing it, looking into it, etcetera. He does this for some time.*

MOKHOVA: [*to* DINSKY] It's your line, Comrade.

DINSKY: I know. I am creating atmosphere. [*He performs a little more cup business, before...*] **Do you think they have nightingales in Galicia, Comrade?**

KAMEV: [*with a slight accent*] **Did you hear a bird?**

DINSKY: **I think so, distantly.**

KAMEV: **It's almost four. Dawn's breaking. The birds will be stirring in the hedgerows.**

DINSKY: **I will have to take your word for it. I am city raised.**

KAMEV: **I didn't know that, Comrade.**

DINSKY: **Oh yes, Moscow, where only the passing clatter of the dust cart or the distant hoot of the factory whistle heralds the new day.** [*Breaking*] I'm coming down, I think. [*He moves downstage.*] **We have pigeons and sparrows and a duck or two on the pond. That is our wildlife. Not much of a dawn chorus!**

KAMEV: **You are lucky, I grew up amid the forests of Samara and on a warm spring morning the dawn chorus can be quite deafening.**

They laugh gently. *(Ha! ha! ha!)*

BABELEV: No, it can't!

KAMEV: Oh yes, we have been out that way, haven't we, Dinsky?

DINSKY: Raucous birdlife.

BABELEV: No, I missed it, he can't come from Samara. Yegorov came from there. We have to change it. Somewhere as far away as possible.

DINSKY: Murmansk!

BABELEV: Perfect. Mokhova, change it from Samara to Murmansk.

MOKHOVA: Everyone make the substitution.

KAMEV: But what about my accent?

BABELEV: I thought you were sucking on something.

DINSKY: Casting your pearls, Leon Grigoryevich.

MOKHOVA: [*clapping her hands*] Your line, Comrade.

KAMEV: Well, for now, I shall refrain from any accent at all. It's beneath me to chase your desperate script changes all over the Motherland. Now… **You are lucky, I grew up in Murmansk and on a warm spring morning the dawn chorus can be quite deafening.**

They laugh gently. *(Ha! ha! ha!)*

DINSKY: [*in character*] I love those warm spring mornings above the Arctic Circle, don't you, Commander?!

They laugh ironically: Ha! ha! ha!

KAMEV: [*breaking*] Oh, indeed! And all that chattering birdlife!

They laugh ironically again: Ha, ha, ha!

BABELEV: Yeah, yeah, yeah—we'll change the line.

KLIMENKO: Ravens—all they have are ravens up there.

NADIA: No, no, they have petrels too. You'll find them out on the marshes, plaintively peeping for their mates—an almost human cry.

DINSKY: Peep-peep.

NADIA: With something rather sad and desperate in the tone, a sense of loss.

DINSKY: [*sadder, with hints of desperation and loss*] Peep-peep.

MOKHOVA: What is the line, Comrade?

BABELEV: We'll go with ravens. So: **You are lucky, I grew up in Murmansk where there were just ravens.** No... **where the ravens could be quite deafening.** Oh, shit!

NADIA: Babelev, please, you are in the theatre.

BABELEV: Sorry... I've got it. **If you think factory whistles are loud, try ravens...** Oh, crap!

KAMEV: Ahh! The Soviet artist at work!

DINSKY: The engineer of human souls applying his wrench!

GLEMOV: Excuse me, Comrade, but what about: 'You are lucky, I grew up in Murmansk and woken each morning to the squawk of ravens—ha! ha! ha!'

BABELEV: That's it. We will go with that.

MOKHOVA: Everyone make the substitution.

KAMEV: Goalies writing the dialogue. Since we're short a director, perhaps we should approach the charlady.

BABELEV: Have you got that, Kamev?

KAMEV: [*writing*] Oh, yes. 'Squawk of ravens—ha! ha! ha!' Are you ready for your entrance, miss?

> BABELEV *reluctantly moves to stage left with* KLIMENKO *and* NADIA.

NADIA: Your upstage ear, if you don't mind.

KLIMENKO: I'm upstage where?

NADIA: No your upstage ear, give it to me.

> KLIMENKO *bends to allow* NADIA *to grab hold of his ear.*

KLIMENKO: Sure, just let me lead with it.

> *They do a practice turn,* NADIA *holding onto* KLIMENKO*'s ear. They exit for their entrance with* BABELEV.

MOKHOVA: [*clapping her hands*] Could we go back to Commander One's line: 'Not much of a dawn chorus!'

DINSKY: **Not much of a dawn chorus!**

KAMEV: **You are lucky, I grew up in Murmansk and every morning woken to the squawk of ravens.**

> *They laugh pointedly. 'Ha, ha, ha!'*

DINSKY: **You were right. I see a little light in the east.** [*Breaking*] **Oops!** I shouldn't have come down. [*He rushes back up to the window.*] *Now*, **I see a little light in the east. The boss will be back soon, we will have to stir the men.**

> ***There is a commotion outside.*** NADIA, KLIMENKO, *and* BABELEV *rhubarb loudly.*

KAMEV: **It seems as if something has stirred them already.**

> *On a silent three count,* NADIA, *as an Old Peasant Woman—bow-legged but tough—enters, pulling* KLIMENKO, *as the Young Soldier, by the ear.* BABELEV, *as the Young Girl, follows.*

NADIA: **Who's in charge here?**

KLIMENKO: **Ow! Let me go!**

NADIA: **Not till I've spoken to him what's in charge.**

KAMEV: **Madam, you can't come bursting into our headquarters like this!**

NADIA: **Well, for one fing it ain't your headquarters, it's Pulinski's old cottage.**

DINSKY: **Unhand that soldier.**

NADIA: **And for another fing, I won't stand for your men stealin' me pataters.**

KLIMENKO: **I wasn't stealing her potatoes!**

KAMEV: **Oh, it's you again, Comrade. You have a habit of getting yourself into scrapes.**

DINSKY: **Let him go, old woman. This young fellow is known to us.**

> ***The Old Woman reluctantly lets the Young Soldier go. He ruefully rubs his ear.***

NADIA: **Don't you 'old woman' me. I want him strung up for lootin'. T' steal a widda's pataters with a Polish winter not two monffs away. 'E might as well jes shoot me on the spot.**

KLIMENKO: **I wasn't stealing her potatoes.**

NADIA: **He was too. Me granddaugh'er 'ere caught 'im at it. She was wrestlin' 'im when I turned up.**

> ***The commanders smile knowingly.***

DINSKY: **Wrestling him were you, young woman?**

BABELEV: [*in a high sweet voice*] **Well, not exactly.**

DINSKY: [***highly amused***] **Not exactly. I see.**

> *Silence. The actors turn to* GLEMOV, *absorbed by his script and his imminent entrance.*

MOKHOVA: **There is the sound of tuneful whistling outside.** That's you, Comrade Glemov.

GLEMOV: What? I have to whistle?

MOKHOVA: Yes, from outside.

> GLEMOV *exits behind the door, left.*

MOKHOVA: [*to* BABELEV] Give the cue again, Comrade. From Young Girl: 'Well not exactly…?'

GLEMOV: [*sticking his head back in*] Sorry, what tune do I…?

BABELEV: Anything you like for now.

GLEMOV: [*his pipe*] Right! Should I use my pipe?

MOKHOVA: No, just with your lips will do.

GLEMOV: Right.

> *He goes again.*

MOKHOVA: [*to* BABELEV] Comrade?

BABELEV: **Well, not exactly.**

DINSKY: [***highly amused***] **Not exactly. I see.**

> GLEMOV, *offstage, whistles the main theme from* Swan Lake. *There are out-of-character glances between the actors at his choice.*

KAMEV: **Well, it sounds as if Comrade Stalin has arrived just in time to sort out this little quarrel.**

> GLEMOV's *whistling continues, The doorknob rattles, but the door doesn't open. He moves into the next phrase of the tune, which has his door-opening exertions in it. Everyone waits.*

MOKHOVA: [*finally*] You can enter any time you like, Comrade.

> *The whistling stops. Then the door flies open to admit* LARISSA YAKONOVA, *early twenties, in a summer frock and high-heeled shoes, in a state of distress.* GLEMOV *enters helplessly a second or two behind her.*

YAKONOVA: [*between sobs*] Oh God! God! God! God! It's awful! It's
    awful!

NADIA: What's the matter, girl? Catch your breath.

MOKHOVA: Comrade Yakonova, you're late.

YAKONOVA: Oh God! Oh God! Oh God! It's awful!

KAMEV: Yes, Larissa, we got that. But what is the matter?

YAKONOVA: Murder! Oh God! Murder!

> *Silence falls except for* YAKONOVA*'s sobs.*
>
> *Lights fall quickly to black.*

END OF ACT ONE

ACT TWO

The same, a few minutes later.

YAKONOVA, *now seated centre, sips a glass of water, recovering. The cast is attentive to her;* MOKHOVA *is not present.*

YAKONOVA: I honestly don't know what made me get so upset, really.

KAMEV: A natural flair for the dramatic, I expect.

NADIA: Kamev, please. She has been through a distressing ordeal.

KAMEV: A natural dramatic flair to which all actors are prone is all I meant.

YAKONOVA: I was perfectly fine when I left Bryusov Lane. And then it sort of crept up on me. And I became all confused and I jumped on the wrong tram. I wound up on a park bench and I don't know how long I sat there. Then I started walking here, but I found that I was walking quicker and quicker, then I was running. In these heels. And I knew I looked silly and suspicious, tottering on these heels in this heat, and crying, but I couldn't help myself. When I reached the stage door I was fine, but I ended up backstage somewhere, in the dark. Then someone started whistling and for some reason that set me off again.

NADIA: It was obviously very traumatic news.

YAKONOVA: Yes, but that's the point. I didn't know her, really. I mean, I met her once when I was a student when she came to our class, but really…

KLIMENKO: Do they know who did it?

> *Silence, then…*

YAKONOVA: Look, I really don't know.

BABELEV: But somebody must have seen something, heard something.

YAKONOVA: All I know is what I was told.

BABELEV: Which was?

YAKONOVA: Just from the neighbours. I came round the corner and there was a crowd outside the flat. And someone recognised me from some show or other and sort of pulled me in and said, 'Dear, isn't it terrible about poor Zina?' And I almost said, 'Zina who?' I mean I didn't know the Meyerholds lived there, really. I was just trying to get to Gorky Street. She must have thought that since I was an actress I must know Zinaida Raikh. Suddenly, I had half this crowd being sympathetic to me, being kind and lovely to me because they thought that I was her friend or something. They pushed this little bald guy at me to tell me what happened. He was the caretaker. Look, I need some more water.

KLIMENKO *fetches water, filling up her glass.*

NADIA: Who would kill that dear girl?

KLIMENKO: Perhaps a theatre lover.

DINSKY: I'm sorry, Klimenko, but that's a bit harsh.

KLIMENKO: Face it, she wasn't that good, was she?

KAMEV: I see, and we are comparing her to what master of the stage?

DINSKY: Perhaps to some Ukrainian Maestro still playing juveniles in his thirties.

KLIMENKO: All I am saying is—fine, she was all right, but she wasn't a patch on Babanova or a half-dozen others.

DINSKY: She was excellent in *The Lady of the Camellias*.

KLIMENKO: Which she performed to death.

BABELEV: Hardly the right expression under the circumstances.

DINSKY: She did a nice line in self-obsessed neurotics.

KLIMENKO: Which wasn't acting.

NADIA: Gentlemen, please! While I don't mind one way or the other if you speak ill of the dead, I think it disgracefully poor taste to review them.

BABELEV: I don't know what this all means.

KLIMENKO: It doesn't mean anything. It was just some thug. He thought: Meyerhold's arrested, his wife's probably still in Leningrad—empty flat, full of choice Party-sanctioned loot. He sneaks up the fire escape and in through the window, but Raikh surprises him—

KAMEV: With a petition.

NADIA: Kamev, decorum please!

KLIMENKO: Anyway, there's a struggle, he grabs the kitchen knife, and a fatal wound. A senseless crime. Meaningless.

YAKONOVA: There were two of them.

KLIMENKO: Two thugs, then. Same difference.

YAKONOVA: She had been in all night, the caretaker told me. Anyone would have seen the lights on if they had been watching the place. About one o'clock he woke up with a commotion upstairs, banging and screaming. So he listened for a while and it fell silent.

NADIA: He should have gone up to see what was going on.

BABELEV: Yes, but nobody does that anymore, do they? I wouldn't have gone up. Would you?

NADIA: Don't be absurd; I'm an old woman. But I would hope that if a thug was assaulting me, someone would come to my aid or at least call the police.

YAKONOVA: It was the police!

Silence. They stare at her.

Oh, God! I shouldn't have said that, really. I should have… I don't know… I don't know that it was the police.

BABELEV: [*to* YAKONOVA] Is that what the caretaker said?

NADIA: I think we should take a break. We are straying into dangerous territory.

YAKONOVA: No, he didn't. I shouldn't have said that… He doesn't really know.

NADIA: If he doesn't know, I don't see much point to empty speculation. Now, I bought in a little cake for all of us to share.

YAKONOVA: All he said was he heard footsteps coming down the fire escape and another set of footsteps bounding down the stairs and the front door slam. So he got out of bed and looked out his window towards Gorky Street. Two men were running towards a big black car waiting for them. They jumped in and it roared off.

MOKHOVA enters upstage. She has valerian in a little bottle. She stops, watches and listens.

BABELEV: It has to be the Cheka.

NADIA: It has to be no such thing.

BABELEV: Well, who else would have a car?

YAKONOVA: Nothing was taken.

KLIMENKO: Which just supports the idea that they were robbers who were disturbed.

YAKONOVA: [*with slowly increasing vehemence*] But they stabbed her so many times. Why stab her so many times? And why the eyes? That's what the caretaker kept saying: 'Why the eyes?' He led me in to see the stairs and there was blood—handprints all the way down the wall where the second guy ran down. And I felt faint and sat on the stairs, and he couldn't stop telling me the story. When the car had gone, he went up to Meyerhold's flat and there she was on the floor—still breathing, but there was so much blood. She seemed to be cut everywhere. Her nightgown was red and shredded...

> *Silence.*

NADIA: Either way, we cannot involve ourselves in such distressing matters.

KLIMENKO: Well, I still don't buy it.

YAKONOVA: She must have already been unconscious or held down when he stabbed her eyes. [*Directly at* KLIMENKO, *almost accusing*] Because how do you stab someone's eyes while they are struggling?

KLIMENKO: [*placating her*] All right. All right.

YAKONOVA: She had to be still! She had to be lying there helpless! You tell me! Why the eyes?

> KLIMENKO, *about to answer, sees* MOKHOVA *and clams up. Silence as all turn to her.*

MOKHOVA: [*to* YAKONOVA] Comrade, I don't think you should say any more. I am sure the authorities will look into it. Now, sit down, please.

> YAKONOVA *sits;* MOKHOVA *unscrews the bottle and pulls out the dropper.*

Open up.

YAKONOVA *opens her mouth and* MOKHOVA *squeezes drops onto her tongue.*

YAKONOVA: [*reacting to the bitterness*] What is it?

MOKHOVA: Valerian—it will calm you down. Stop you getting excited and saying silly things. Everyone can help by not encouraging you.

YAKONOVA: I just need to freshen up.

MOKHOVA: An excellent idea. Nadia and one of you Comrades, could you help her to the dressing-room? We'll have a fifteen-minute break and then resume.

She claps her hands.

NADIA: I thought we could have a glass of tea and a piece of the cake I brought in.

MOKHOVA: Yes, we can have that, but straight after we must go back to work. I will see if the boy's returned yet.

MOKHOVA *exits.*

NADIA: Let's get her to the dressing-room. Glemov?

GLEMOV: Right-o.

GLEMOV *and* NADIA *help* YAKONOVA *from her chair and head upstage.*

YAKONOVA: I'm sorry. I don't know why I am like this, really, because I didn't know her.

NADIA: For an actor, it can be shocking to hear of a death in the theatre family.

GLEMOV: You'll be all right.

YAKONOVA: I'm sorry, who are you?

NADIA: Glemov is playing Comrade Stalin, dear.

YAKONOVA: I thought you weren't in until Wednesday.

NADIA: The woman below him cooks cabbage.

GLEMOV: Well, that's not quite the whole story. You see—

YAKONOVA: [*stopping and turning*] Where's Trifinov?

NADIA: He's just late.

YAKONOVA: He's not here?

DINSKY: Mokhova has sent the boy to his flat.

YAKONOVA: He's an hour late.

KLIMENKO: And then some. He'll be getting a hell of a report from Comrade Stage Manager.

YAKONOVA: Oh God, something's happened to him.

DINSKY: Oh, no, no. It was a big night. He's just overslept.

YAKONOVA: Something's happened. I know it. Maybe they came for him too.

NADIA: Now, now, calm down, my dear. No-one has come for anyone. [*To* GLEMOV] Take her arm. Come on, dear.

YAKONOVA: [*breaking away*] He should be here.

KLIMENKO: He forgot to wind up his alarm clock.

BABELEV: Yeah, yeah, but what if this is the start of something? First Meyerhold, now Raikh.

KLIMENKO: Don't start, Babelev.

BABELEV: [*to* YAKONOVA] Look, I don't think Trifinov was taken, Larissa. He'll turn up, I'm sure. But what if this is the start of something? You know, a…

KLIMENKO: A purge, oh, no.

BABELEV: Or a… whatever. You know how these things are. They come down on a group, don't they? Run a scythe through the engineers, the army, or the poets. Maybe they are coming down on the theatre.

KLIMENKO: The purges are over.

BABELEV: Who said? Meyerhold was taken, Babel was taken, and Koltsov. All in the last couple of months.

KLIMENKO: Babel and Koltsov are writers.

BABELEV: Yeah, yeah, and what am I? A bowl of borscht? If they have targeted artists—

KLIMENKO: Three people do not make a purge.

BABELEV: Then a mini-purge.

KLIMENKO: Oh, a purge-ette. You mean not a complete flush of the system, more like a sudden bowel movement.

NADIA: Gentlemen, please!

BABELEV: Don't mock me, Ukrainian. Just the top guys.

KLIMENKO: So why should that worry you?

BABELEV: I've had two hits in a row.

KAMEV: The reviews from last night haven't come out yet, Babelev.

DINSKY: Which only makes one hit in a row.

KAMEV: Not technically a string of success.

DINSKY: A bead of success.

YAKONOVA: They have taken Trifinov, I know it.

KLIMENKO: [*to* BABELEV] See, Comrade, you are stirring up Yakonova again.

KAMEV: [*to* YAKONOVA] We don't know enough to say that, my dear.

KLIMENKO: Believe us, Larrisa, he has less to fear than Babelev here.

NADIA: Frankly, gentlemen, I think this discussion is getting far too political.

BABELEV: It is not a political discussion. It is an artistic one.

KLIMENKO: He's right. We are discussing whether Comrades Babelev and Trifinov have what it takes to incur the wrath of the NKVD. I say no. I mean, pick the odd man out: Isaac Babel, one of the greatest short story writers Russia has ever produced; Mikhail Koltsov, hero journalist of the Spanish Civil War; Vsevolod Meyerhold, world-renowned director of the Meyerhold Theatre; and Dimitri Babelev, author of… [*tip of the tongue*] mmm… of…

KAMEV: *Precision Milled.*

BABELEV: Oh, screw you! Both of you.

KLIMENKO: Thank you. *Precision Milled.* Oh, good God, Babelev! Look at you! You're getting sulky because the secret police have no reason to arrest you. Look, pal, I'm not knocking your work, really. But if they are coming after the great artists of the Soviet Union, they're not coming after you. Or Trifinov either. I am sorry, Larissa, but I can't see the Chekists being interested in him.

YAKONOVA: He's a distinguished director.

KLIMENKO: You haven't been in the business long.

YAKONOVA: He is an artist!

Silence.

KLIMENKO: Please, don't all rush to speak at once.

DINSKY: He is not without skill.

KAMEV: [*to* YAKONOVA] I must say that I have watched how Trifinov has taken you under his wing over the last few weeks, Larissa Sergeyevna, but the tutelage of an older man can be an overpowering experience for a young, impressionable person, and can blind you to his limitations.

DINSKY: He's very good with sets.

NADIA: In the broad sense, of course he is an artist.

KLIMENKO: But I think it was in the narrow sense that she was speaking.

NADIA: Well, directors, my dear, come in three general types: the brilliant ones who inspire you to greatness; the bad ones who are destructive of talent; and the vast majority who are, I suppose, like homeopaths: what they prescribe can't possibly do you any good, yet on the other hand, there is little prospect of serious harm.

YAKONOVA: And that's Stephan Platonovich?

NADIA: A genial dispenser of sugar pills, I'm afraid.

DINSKY: And that's not to say he has no talent. As I said, he's great with sets, and he blocks quite… quickly.

KLIMENKO: Occasionally he'll suggest something that's right on the money.

DINSKY: He's not brilliant, but so few of us are. We all have our little talents which we finesse as impressively as we can.

KAMEV: Naturally, some are blessed more than others.

DINSKY: Oh, I don't know. Most of us are just making up the numbers.

KAMEV: You are surely not speaking for yourself, old friend?

DINSKY: Oh, I have no illusions, I am not one of the great ones. But there are not that many of them around. In acting, I don't know, at any one time, maybe two or three. Ilinsky would be one.

KLIMENKO: Knipper.

NADIA: Babanova.

DINSKY: Oh, yes. Well, there's your three. Who else is there?

KAMEV: Frankly, I find such comparisons tedious.

DINSKY: I mean, Babanova's Juliet, who saw that? A little too old for the part, but, by golly, everything she did seemed fresh and delicate as a young girl in love.

NADIA: In my day it was Kommisarshevskaya. I worked with her as a young actor and spent every performance in the wings watching her.

DINSKY: And all I'm saying is that most of us, we who are talented, merely talented, talented enough to make our lives in the theatre, struggle to create our occasional magic, failing as often as we succeed. I work up a little business with my cane and get a bit of attention, but the rest of my performance will be forgotten pretty quickly. I know it. But a few, the very blessed, like Babanova, have it to burn.

KAMEV: I think we have strayed from the subject.

BABELEV: Yeah, yeah, yeah, talent's got nothing to do with it anyway. Sure, they have snatched the big guys, but that is how it works. Start at the top and work the way down. In '37, in the Writers' Union they arrested the stars and the bureaucrats first, but pretty quickly it didn't matter who it was: translators, editors, poets—God!—proofreaders! In the end they were snatching copyboys.

KLIMENKO: But that's over.

BABELEV: It's started again.

NADIA: Klimenko is right. As I understand it, and I have not a few slight contacts in the know, the Terror is over. There had been a serious problem with Trotsky trying to undermine the country's achievements and, unfortunately, too much zeal was applied to thwart the villain's efforts. I have it on good authority that they are only going after the major enemies of the State now.

YAKONOVA: And was Zinaida Raikh a major enemy of the State?

NADIA: Now that Comrade Beria is Head of Internal Security things will be far less chaotic.

YAKONOVA: [*with rising anger*] Far less chaotic! With Zinaida Raikh lying in a pool of blood, with her eyes gouged out? Was she a major enemy of State?

NADIA: Don't shout, girl. I won't be shouted at in the theatre.

KLIMENKO: We don't know it was the Chekists.

BABELEV: It was the Chekists. Believe me, it was a warning.

KLIMENKO: A warning of what, Babelev?

BABELEV: How should I know, for Pete's sake? Do I speak their language? Do I understand their inscrutable jargon of blood and fear? Maybe it is a warning to wives that says: 'If your husband goes missing in the night don't kick up a stink, don't go pestering members of the Politburo with your petitions.' Or maybe it's saying: 'Yes, it is true that the Terror is over, but our claws are only retracted. See! We can swipe out like this whenever we like.'

NADIA: Oh, this is absurd!

BABELEV: Yeah, yeah, well, I'm sorry, Nadia, if this seems silly to you. Obviously, we ordinary folk would be much calmer if we had friends among the Party bosses.

NADIA: I have acquaintanceships—not friendships—in the leadership, mainly through my late husband, who was a respected member of the Party and performed loyal service.

BABELEV: Oh, yes, we'll have all heard a few things about your husband's loyal service. From what I hear, some very enthusiastic Party work in Armenia in '29.

NADIA: I do not know what you are implying, simply because I made it a rule never to question Victor on Party business. It was none of my affair. And nor should it be yours!

BABELEV: No, you don't ask questions. Why should you when keeping your mouth shut gets you a nice apartment by the river and a dacha by the sea?

KLIMENKO: [*coming to* NADIA*'s defence*] Hey, hey, hey, pal…

NADIA: This is crass of you, Babelev. This is just not done. Victor's death left me a few residual privileges, which I accept gratefully as a widow of a certain age.

KLIMENKO: You have gone too far, Babelev. You need to apologise.

NADIA: I don't need an apology, but we should get this girl to the dressing-rooms so that she can calm down. So we can all calm down. There has been a lot of foolishness spoken that were it reported would get us all into trouble. We will have a little cake and tea. Babelev, I'm sorry, but you are not invited.

All exit, except BABELEV *and* GLEMOV.

GLEMOV *mooches around the stage, looking at bits of the set, opening doors and draws, picking up tools, etcetera. A silence.*

BABELEV: Aren't you going for cake?

GLEMOV: I'm in training.

BABELEV: But you're injured.

GLEMOV: Coach's orders.

BABELEV: Do you always do what your coach tells you?

GLEMOV: Yeah, pretty much. Simplifies things.

BABELEV: In what way?

GLEMOV: Well, for one thing, you don't waste time thinking about cake. [*The brickwork on the factory set*] Hey, these bricks are terrific! You have to get right up to them to see that they're not real.

BABELEV: The magic of theatre. [*Pause.*] We're not normally this argumentative, you know.

GLEMOV: It didn't seem that bad.

BABELEV: It's only that Klimenko's a prick! Smart-arse! [*Pause.*] It must be the same in football, when you and your team mates have arguments.

GLEMOV: Are you going to shag his wife and piss in his boots?

BABELEV: [*shocked at the suggestion*] No!

GLEMOV: Not quite the same, then.

> *Pause.*

BABELEV: I probably overreacted. I can't seem to control my nerves. I take deep breaths but it doesn't really help.

GLEMOV: You have to use your nerves.

BABELEV: What do you mean?

GLEMOV: [*after a second's thought*] I'm not sure. It's just what we say in football before a big game, the coach tells us: 'Use those nerves!'

BABELEV: How?

GLEMOV: He never says. I jump up and down on my six-yard line—that usually does the trick. You should try it.

BABELEV: I'd never stop jumping. I would have jumped every waking moment these last two years.

GLEMOV: [*with a chisel*] Hey, this is a wood chisel; this is no good for metalwork.

BABELEV: Well, we're not the Moscow Art Theatre, are we? [*Beat.*] I haven't had a decent night's sleep since '36. The Cheka was always stomping up our stairs.

GLEMOV: Right.

BABELEV: We'd lie together in our bed holding our breaths as they came closer and closer, louder and louder. And Annushka would whisper, 'I bet you they'll stop at the fifth, Dimitri.' And I'd say, 'A kopek and a kiss says the sixth.' We were on the seventh, you see. And she was always right. The footsteps would stop in front of some other poor bastard's flat and I would kiss Annushka and she'd say, 'That's nine kopeks you owe me', and we would try to fall asleep with our hearts racing.

GLEMOV: Sleep like a log, me. All the training. [*Beat.*] I thought you didn't sleep with your wife?

BABELEV: Yeah, yeah, yeah, but, you know. [*Pause.*] Actually—but don't tell anyone, you have to promise, I mean, you can't tell anyone, all right?

GLEMOV: Sure.

BABELEV: What I said about all that, before, isn't strictly true.

GLEMOV: You're not divorced?

BABELEV: Oh, yeah, yeah, yeah, but we got divorced when I was a poet and they were snatching a lot of poets, and they sometimes snatched the wives as well, and the kids, or kicked them out of their apartments, so we divorced. Best thing really.

GLEMOV: Right.

BABELEV: Don't tell anyone.

GLEMOV: Oh, no.

BABELEV: It is a sort of divorce of convenience. Since things had quietened down, we were thinking of getting married again. But then the theatre calls and says, 'What about writing a play about Stalin for his sixtieth birthday?' And I say, 'Love to!'—like an idiot.

GLEMOV: It sounds like a great honour.

BABELEV: It's a nightmare. The theatre wants to vet every draft, the Writers' Union is looking over your shoulder, the Artistic Affairs people send you long lists of things you are not allowed to mention.

GLEMOV: Like what?

BABELEV: You know, Stalin's smallpox scars, for one; his dodgy left arm. I'm still waiting to hear back about the moustache. It's like having fifty coaches telling you what to do and, believe me, it simplifies nothing. Because not one of them knows what they're talking about. They're just shit-scared they will fail to ban something that someone further up the chain decides needs banning. I should have stayed a poet.

GLEMOV: [*pointing to the wall*] Is that your slogan?

BABELEV: No, Stalin wrote that one.

GLEMOV: No, I mean, when you write the play, do you have to say what slogan you want?

BABELEV: No, they generally use what's going. I just write: 'Curtain rises on a ball-bearing factory', and they pull the factory set out of stock, changing the slogan so it isn't instantly recognisable from the last time a play was set in a factory.

GLEMOV: And when was that?

BABELEV: You don't go to the theatre much, do you?

GLEMOV: No.

BABELEV: [*suddenly exploding*] They are set in a factory all the fucking time!

GLEMOV: Oh.

BABELEV: Or a hydro power plant, or a foundry, or a collective farm, or on the civil war front—all the places in the world I have no experience of, but which I am expected to recreate to the life.

GLEMOV: I see.

BABELEV: For Pete's sake! [*Taking control of himself*] I'm sorry, I'm sorry. I didn't mean to shout at you. Because I think you are perfect, you know that, for this role, Stalin, just perfect.

GLEMOV: Thanks.

BABELEV: The moment Trifinov told me about you, I thought, 'That's a bloody stroke of genius!'

GLEMOV: Why?

BABELEV: Because the Artistic Affairs guys have to accept you. They have to. Look at you—big, brawny, Nordic. These guys choke on the smallest crumb of truth, but they'll open their gullets wide for a big fat lie. I mean, none of them will say, 'Hey, he's too tall for Stalin', will they? Because that's the same as saying Stalin is short.

GLEMOV: [*confused*] And he's not short?

BABELEV: Not officially. So, you're fine. I don't have to worry about you. Just everything else. [*He takes a few deep breaths.*] I mean, first this Yegerov problem and Zinaida Raikh and now maybe Trifinov. I just feel they're coming my way. [*More deep breaths.*] This is how they do it, bit by bit, just working on your nerves. This is how they whittle you down.

> *He starts pacing and breathing.*

GLEMOV: Are you all right?

BABELEV: Yeah, yeah, yeah—just a small panic attack. I have them all the time. If they can do it to Meyerhold, you know. Biggest guy in town. Too big to chop down in one hit, so chip, chip, chip. Condemned his shows, then condemned his theatre, then condemned him. At the directors' conference last month, he stood there apologising for his errors he knew he never committed. We knew he never committed. Stooped, shuffling his papers. A great oak turned to firewood and kindling. Chopped down to size so they could just back up the van and chuck him in.

GLEMOV: Does anyone know what happened to him?

BABELEV: Ask Beria.

GLEMOV: [*seriously*] It doesn't sound like something I could ask him.

BABELEV: [*rhetorically, with increasing anger*] Yeah, yeah, just walk up to him and ask him straight: Where's Meyerhold? What the hell have you done with him? And while you're at it, where's Babel? And Pilnyak and Mandelstam? What have you done with our literature? Yeah, and ask him what did Zinaida Raikh ever do to deserve being carved up like a pig on a hook?

GLEMOV: Umm, I—I don't think I can ask him any of those questions.

BABELEV: No.

> *A silence on realising that* GLEMOV *is saying he knows Beria. A shock.*

You know Beria?

GLEMOV: Oh, yeah. Not very well, but, you know, enough to say hello to.

BABELEV: You say hello to the Head of Soviet Security?

GLEMOV: He's a big Dinamo fan. Likes to pop his head into the dressing-room before a game, that sort of thing. Keeps slapping me on the back all the time and calling me Gleb.

BABELEV: And what do you call him?

GLEMOV: Comrade Commissar Beria. I mean, we're not pals or anything. But he got me this job here.

BABELEV: I thought Trifinov cast you. He said you auditioned.

GLEMOV: I really don't know how these things work. Beria phoned me at home and said he was sorry I broke my arm, but don't worry, he had a special project lined up for me. And a few days later I met Trifinov and what's-his-name, the theatre manager, upstairs, and this other guy.

BABELEV: What guy?

GLEMOV: I don't know who he was. He seemed official. He didn't take off his coat. He just sat in the corner and smiled the whole time.

BABELEV: [*sotto*] Oh, my God!

> BABELEV *starts taking deep breaths.*

GLEMOV: I said straight out, I didn't know anything about acting, and this smiling guy said it didn't matter. And Trifinov agreed and said they would set me up with a good acting coach, so I was fine about it. 'Cause I work well with a good coach.

BABELEV: [*sotto*] Oh, my God!

GLEMOV: Then I shook Trifinov's hand, and the manager guy's.

BABELEV: And the smiling guy?

GLEMOV: No, he just picked up his hat and walked out.

BABELEV: Oh, God! [*Beat.*] Have you been sent?

GLEMOV: What?

BABELEV: By the Cheka. Are you Beria's man? Are you making a report?!

GLEMOV: No, no. I was just told to do the play.

BABELEV: Don't lie. The things I've said! The things I've told you! Are you a spy?

GLEMOV: No.

BABELEV: If you do anything that hurts my wife and kid.

GLEMOV: Honestly, I wouldn't. I wouldn't.

BABELEV: No?

GLEMOV: No. I'm a goalie.

BABELEV: [*vaguely, as if in shock*] All right. All right. Good. So, Artistic Affairs, the Head of Soviet Security and, of course, Stalin, are all taking a personal interest in my play. My play. That's really flattering when you come to think about it. Can't wait for opening night.

> BABELEV *laughs lightly then, slowly at first but with increasing vigour, he starts to jump up and down on the spot.* GLEMOV *watches for a while.*

GLEMOV: Is it working?

> BABELEV *shakes his head.* DINSKY *enters with a glass of tea and the last of his cake on a saucer, and joins* GLEMOV *watching* BABELEV.

Well, keep jumping. Believe me, it does the trick. [*To* DINSKY] How's the cake?

DINSKY: Pretty good, walnut, though it needs a little butter to go with it.

> KAMEV *with* YAKONOVA *enter.*

KAMEV: Now you see, a performance of a play is a string of moments, do you understand? Now, my late wife, Rula Leshkova, she always said, 'The theatrical moment is pure'.

YAKONOVA: [*suspicions aroused*] Aha.

KAMEV: Every moment of the play, you ask yourself, what is happening now? What is the main objective? And what can I do to keep it pure?

YAKONOVA: Aha.

KAMEV: Purity, you see. Now, you have so much to learn, but if an old stager may be permitted to impart one lesson invaluable in your future career, it is this idea of the pure theatrical moment.

YAKONOVA: I'm not changing the red hankie business, Kamev.

KAMEV: No, that's not what I am talking about. Well, that is actually only partly what I am talking about. A case in point, in fact, because you are, you must admit, pulling focus from the main objective of the scene. But the general concept, you see…

YAKONOVA: Trifinov told me to do it.

KAMEV: [*getting worked up*] Yes? Well, I'm afraid—all my respects to him—but he has made a basic error. Because you do not have someone pouring out his passion on one part of the stage and have someone doing something distracting and completely irrelevant on the other.

YAKONOVA: Trifinov told me to do it and that's that.

> YAKONOVA *joins* DINSKY *and* GLEMOV.

KAMEV: You sullied my moment!

> KAMEV *storms upstage to the table and sits.* NADIA *and* KLIMENKO *enter.*

KLIMENKO: I think with all this rationing will anyone know how to bake cakes and biscuits if it carries on for much longer?

NADIA: Fortunately, my late husband had a sweet tooth, so the recipes have become part of the wood.

KLIMENKO: He was a lucky man. And you managed to get your hands on some sugar, I see.

NADIA: Oh, nothing more than a widow's meagre ration saved over a few weeks, supplemented by some molasses I found at the bottom of an old tin and a serendipitous egg.

KLIMENKO: And some serendipitous flour and quite a few serendipitous walnuts.

NADIA: They were things I had in stock, old stock, that's all. Is that the play's author I see jumping up and down?

KLIMENKO: Yes, it is. No, I was just thinking that if you ever have an urge to do more baking, I might be able to cobble together a few ingredients for you.

NADIA: We are not having prematurely the conversation that I firmly postponed until luncheon, are we?

> BABELEV *stops jumping, out of breath and sweating.*

KLIMENKO: No, no, you know me…

NADIA: Thank heavens, he's stopped.

DINSKY: Well done.

GLEMOV: Feel better?

BABELEV: I feel hot.

NADIA: A predictable consequence. Now, if you don't mind my saying so, I feel that these rehearsals have strayed from their proper path. First with tragic news, then with politics and [*pointedly at* KLIMENKO] commerce, and now with extemporised gymnastics.

DINSKY: Yes, we should keep rehearsing, at least until things sort themselves out.

NADIA: Now, we're walking it through. Are you up to it, Larissa dear?

YAKONOVA: Yes, I think so.

KLIMENKO: Keep ourselves occupied until Trifinov turns up.

> DINSKY *has poured* BABELEV *a glass of water and gives it to him.*

BABELEV: Thanks.

DINSKY: And our author, after his exertions, can sit out this time. Larissa, he was an excellent Polish farm girl. A few more minutes and he would have walked off with your part!

> *The joke dies. One by one, the cast pick up their scripts, except* KAMEV, *who is in a funk.*

YAKONOVA: [*now with her replacement pages*] What scene?

KLIMENKO: Seven. Just as Stalin enters.

NADIA: Should we take Stalin's whistling as read?

DINSKY & KLIMENKO: [*together*] Please.

GLEMOV: I had a problem with the door.

DINSKY: Are you joining us, Comrade Commander?

KAMEV: I was thinking of staying here, way upstage, and delivering my lines loudly while waving my arms around.

DINSKY: Now, now, now. Up you get, Leon Grigoryevich.

KAMEV: Whatever happened to the ideal of the ensemble, Dinsky? Each of us playing our respective instruments in harmony?

YAKONOVA: What's he going on about now?

DINSKY: Oh, nothing.

KAMEV: [*rising*] Nothing that need concern you. The passing of standards, that's all. They passed long before your time.

YAKONOVA: And whose standards might they be?

DINSKY: [*heading off trouble*] Oh, no, no, no, no.

YAKONOVA: Old blow-hard standards? Old has-been standards?

DINSKY: [*feeling the blow*] Oooh! Now, now, now.

KAMEV: Oh, let her speak, Dinsky. Because the thing that gets my goat is not being upstaged, but that she is not even good at it. I mean, a red cloth! What happened? Couldn't you find a flashing light? Or a Claxton horn? You are so obvious, little girl.

YAKONOVA: Oh, little girl! Ha!

KAMEV: My wife, Rula Leshkova, now there was a *woman*, a real artist and, bless her soul and Dinsky will bear me out, a hell of an upstager.

DINSKY: Ah, yes, the best!

KAMEV: She could raise her eyebrow, her *eyebrow*, and you'd be drawn to watching her—and nothing and no-one else.

DINSKY: That eyebrow could pull focus from a battle scene.

KLIMENKO: Oh, yeah, yeah, right! [*He laughs.*] There was giants in them days and all that!

KAMEV *suddenly grabs him by the shirt front, hot with rage.*

KAMEV: What are you saying about her?

KLIMENKO: Hey! Hey!

KAMEV: About my dead wife?

KLIMENKO: I said, nothing.

DINSKY: He didn't mean anything. [*Pause.*] Leon Grigoryevich. [*Pause.*] Lev. [*Pause.*] Chum.

KAMEV *and* KLIMENKO, *frozen, stare at each other.* MOKHOVA *has entered, strangely subdued.*

MOKHOVA: [*calmly, firmly*] Let him go, Comrade.

No-one moves.

Let him go, please.

KAMEV: [*letting him go, passion spent*] Certainly. I'm sorry.

KLIMENKO: Let's forget it.

NADIA: Oh, thank heaven!

KAMEV: [*recovering, to* YAKONOVA] See, there you go. The pure theatrical moment. Everyone speaking their lines, but the focus right at the centre of the action.

DINSKY: Glass of water, Leon Grigoryevich?

KAMEV *nods.*

Oh, this heat is making everyone fractious!

DINSKY *pours* KAMEV *a glass of water.*

NADIA: Have we found our director, dear?

MOKHOVA: He's not at his flat. The woman across the hall let Mischa in and he hadn't slept there last night. His wife and little girls are visiting relatives in the country.

BABELEV: Maybe, he was picked up on his way home.

KLIMENKO: Dear God, Babelev!

BABELEV: Well, we should start thinking about such possibilities.

MOKHOVA: Let's eliminate all other possibilities first, Comrade. I have informed upstairs and they're phoning hospitals.

YAKONOVA: Oh!

MOKHOVA: Does anyone know when he left last night?

DINSKY: He was still here at midnight when we left. Isn't that right, Leon Grigoryevich?

KAMEV: By the bar.

KLIMENKO: Yeah, that's right, chatting to that Moskfilm actress, Buslaeva. I saw them. But they'd gone by half-twelve when they chucked us out.

KAMEV: Well, that solves that mystery. Does anyone have this Buslaeva's address? No doubt we will find him there, exhausted from a long night's discussion of montage.

YAKONOVA: He wouldn't do that.

KAMEV: Why not? His wife and kids are in the country, opening night went well, that would have put him in a good mood, and we all know of his abiding interest in cinematic technique.

DINSKY: Now, now, Kamev.

KAMEV: There would have been no impediment to a little tryst.

YAKONOVA: He wouldn't do that.

KAMEV: He is no saint, my dear.

YAKONOVA: He didn't do that.

KAMEV: Oh, and you know that, do you?

YAKONOVA: Yes.

KAMEV: Your faith in faithless man is touching.

YAKONOVA: Because he was with me.

KAMEV: Oh, I see.

YAKONOVA: All night!

> YAKONOVA *is horrified by what she had admitted. Silence.*

MOKHOVA: When did you see him last?

KAMEV: What was I saying about the passing of standards, Dinsky?

> KAMEV *moves upstage, pleased with himself.* YAKONOVA *stands in embarrassed shock. A silence.*

MOKHOVA: Comrade? [*She claps her hands.*] Comrade?

YAKONOVA: Yes, yes—um—this morning, about seven.

MOKHOVA: Where was he going?

YAKONOVA: This is…

MOKHOVA: [*firmly*] Where?

YAKONOVA: Back to his flat to clean up and change and then here. He had a bit to do before rehearsals.

MOKHOVA: Well, there's no sign he ever got here.

BABELEV: They were waiting for him in his flat.

KLIMENKO: Oh, bloody hell! You have started him off again!

BABELEV: Or waiting for him as he left Larissa's.

KLIMENKO: Anything could have happened to him.

BABELEV: For him to be an hour and a half late for rehearsals?

KLIMENKO: I don't know. Knocked down by a truck.

YAKONOVA: [*horrified*] Oh, my God!

KLIMENKO: Or—or a—a bicycle.

KAMEV: A big bicycle, obviously.

MOKHOVA: [*clapping her hands*] Let's just stop there, please, Comrades. We are phoning the hospitals.

BABELEV: Yeah, yeah, but not the police.

MOKHOVA: I don't think that there is a need for that yet.

BABELEV: Why not? That's what you do, don't you? Someone goes missing, you give the cops a call. See if there has been any report of an accident. They'd know. But we don't call them, not when we think they could have had something to do with it.

MOKHOVA: Comrade! What you are saying can get you into trouble.

NADIA: I think we all could get in hot water just listening to him.

KLIMENKO: We could definitely get bored listening to him.

BABELEV: If you're so certain that he hasn't been picked up, Klimenko, give the Cheka a call?

KLIMENKO: Mokhova's got it under control.

BABELEV: Yeah, of course they'll want to know your name first and why you are calling.

KLIMENKO: It's being dealt with.

BABELEV: Our director goes missing the same day that thugs murder one of our top actresses. Almost a month to the day that her husband, the famous Meyerhold, gets carted away by the Chekists. And you think it can be no more than a coincidence. How can you be so sure that they haven't swooped on every theatre in town, picking up directors and actors? How can you be sure that the vans haven't just pulled up outside this very theatre?

KLIMENKO: I can't, but I am sure paranoid hysteria won't help.

BABELEV: Believe me, we paranoid hysterics are the seers of this new age. Whatever we imagine, comes true.

MOKHOVA: [clapping her hands] That's a reportable statement, Comrade.

BABELEV: So what about it, Klimenko?

MOKHOVA: I must put an end to this discussion right now. [She claps her hands.] Please, Comrades!

BABELEV: And stop that bloody clapping, for Pete's sake! It drives us nuts! [To KLIMENKO] Can we send you upstairs to make the call?

KLIMENKO: No. All right, all right, I guess, it's a possibility.

YAKONOVA: Oh, no!

BABELEV: At last!

KLIMENKO: Yeah, but just a possibility. There's a hundred other things that could have happened to him first. But, you know, these are strange times.

MOKHOVA: Enough! [Clapping her hands] You cannot say that these are strange times!

DINSKY: Well, all times have their strangeness.

MOKHOVA: All except these times, Comrade.

GLEMOV: Yes, but in that case, wouldn't that then make them very strange indeed?

MOKHOVA: [*flustered*] No more. Comrades, we are going to rehearse from where we left off—scene—scene—after Stalin's entrance, what's that?

DINSKY: Seven.

MOKHOVA: Seven. Page—page—you know what the page is. To your places.

She claps her hands.

NADIA: You know, my dear, he does have a point about the clapping.

The cast reluctantly pick up their scripts and begin to move into position.

YAKONOVA: Where am I supposed to be?

NADIA: By me, child, over here, but watch my legs.

YAKONOVA: What's wrong with them?

NADIA: Rickets.

YAKONOVA: It feels wrong going ahead without Trifinov. It's as if we have accepted that something's happened to him, so we are already making do without him.

NADIA: Hush now. We must work. Remember, child, the worst catastrophes never leave the imagination.

YAKONOVA: I don't know if I can do this without Trifinov.

KAMEV: Well, we all understand how you like to do it with Trifinov.

YAKONOVA: [*turning on* KAMEV] You have no right to sneer at me.

KAMEV: My dear, I am not sneering.

MOKHOVA: [*firmly, but ineffectually, trying not to clap*] We will rehearse now.

YAKONOVA: You've been sniggering up your sleeve for the last week. 'The tutelage of an experienced man can be overpowering for a impressionable young actress!' What sort of slimy double-talk was that? You're scandalised, like some old gossip! 'Oh, Larissa Yakonova has taken up with the director! Oh, heavens! How perfectly slutty!'

KAMEV: [*to everyone else*] You see, you correct a fellow artist on a simple a matter of stage etiquette—

MOKHOVA: Comrades, please!

YAKONOVA: You're a joke, Kamev, a joke. You're like some long-winded theatrical anecdote that goes on and on and doesn't have a point.

KAMEV: Oh, how droll, how uncharacteristically droll. I've an ear for second-hand dialogue, and that line's not one of yours, is it?

YAKONOVA: No, actually it's Trifinov's. He said it while we were lying in bed last night.

> *During the following* KAMEV *walks down to the edge of the stage, trying to keep his composure, and looks out to the audience.*

KAMEV: And I was the subject of your post-coital murmurings! I'm moved by the honour.

YAKONOVA: Oh, we love to talk about people like you, Kamev, because you're endlessly amusing. All you old farts from the bourgeois theatre days.

KAMEV: Having no sense of tradition or craft, you wouldn't understand.

YAKONOVA: Oh, we understand, Kamev. That's what makes it so funny. That you think finding the best light to stand in is part of a craft. And that an artistic discussion is ticking someone off: 'Now, now, darling, not so fast with your line, you're stepping on my laugh!' Shtick and ego—that's all your tradition amounts to. And then you have the gall to lecture me about 'the purity of the theatrical moment'! Which when you boil it down is just about the purity of *your* theatrical moment—what can be pulled from *your* bag of tricks that will make the audience look at *you*.

KAMEV: So, I have developed performance techniques, what of it? It is a carpenter's little techniques that stop him from botching the job.

YAKONOVA: No, tricks, tricks. Yes, like walking downstage during someone else's speech to mug at the audience! Look at you! You do it without thinking. You even do it when there's no audience.

DINSKY: Ha! Ha! She's got you there, Leon Grigoryevich.

KLIMENKO: For God's sake, can we move on!

DINSKY: Yes, let me declare the debate between youth and experience an honourable draw.

KAMEV: [*moving upstage, rattled*] Oh, shut up, Dinsky! I would not give this girl one of my hard-won techniques for all her easy theatre school theory.

YAKONOVA: At least at theatre school there was some passion, some belief in the power of theatre. When I came here I couldn't believe my eyes. I said to Trifinov, 'What's wrong with these people! They are all dead on their feet.'

KAMEV: And Trifinov enlightened you, did he? A man who has churned out Soviet potboilers his entire career.

YAKONOVA: You don't know him.

BABELEV: What do you mean 'potboilers'?

YAKONOVA: He's actually passionate about theatre, truly passionate. With ideas. He knows for the time being he has to direct crap—

KAMEV: Ideas?

BABELEV: Crap?

YAKONOVA: Yes, ideas, brilliant ideas. You should hear him talk. Do you think he doesn't know what dreck Socialist Realism is?

MOKHOVA: [*warning*] Comrade…

YAKONOVA: But instead of moaning about it like you, he sees it as a way forward, the step theatre has to make, with all its errors, so a new theatre can be born.

KAMEV: God in heaven! The cant and the clichés! She's worse than the wireless. Turn her off!

YAKONOVA: One that takes the lessons of Socialist Realism and the best parts of Meyerhold to make a truly proletarian theatre.

KAMEV: Meyerhold? [*Pause. Everyone goes quiet.*] Oh, we have a secret admirer of Vsevolod Emileovich! It's all becoming clear now. The mystery of the missing director. Now we know why the Cheka picked him up.

YAKONOVA: You bastard, Kamev!

YAKONOVA *lunges at* KAMEV *who does his best to defend himself.*

KAMEV: Get her off me!

MOKHOVA *and* DINSKY *try to tear them apart, but* YAKONOVA *holds on.*

MOKHOVA: Comrade, please!

YAKONOVA: Bastard! Bourgeois bullshitting bastard!

KAMEV: Ah! Ah! Her fingernails!

DINSKY: Now, Larrisa! Maybe, Glemov, if you don't mind…

GLEMOV: What? Oh, right.

GLEMOV *strides in. He lifts* YAKONOVA *at the waist and hauls her away.*

YAKONOVA: [*as a parting shot*] We planned it, Kamev, the red hankie! Just our little bit of fun for opening night. He said, 'Pull it out in his speech and watch the old fart go crazy!' You're so bloody predictable.

KAMEV: [*examining himself, shaken*] Look at my arm! Look at it! You've drawn blood!

YAKONOVA: Good!

KAMEV: And good for you when Trifinov breaks down in interrogation and spills the beans on all your dramaturgical pillow talk.

YAKONOVA: He wouldn't… [*To* GLEMOV, *who is still holding on to her.*] Let me go!

She struggles away and takes a swipe at GLEMOV, *but hits his plaster cast.*

Aaaaa-oww!

KAMEV: No, he wouldn't, you're right. Because they torture artists so lightly in the Lubyanka. But best be on the safe side: lock your windows and hide your kitchen knives!

The remark hurts more than her sore hand. YAKONOVA *suddenly breaks down and cries, slumping in a chair.* MOKHOVA, NADIA *and* BABELEV *see to her.*

KLIMENKO: Oh, look what you have done, Kamev.

DINSKY: A little callous, old friend.

KAMEV: She attacked me! Everyone is attacking me. What have I done?

BABELEV: [*to* MOKHOVA] Maybe you should give her more valerian.

KAMEV: Double the dose. The last had no effect. Look at my arm!

MOKHOVA: [*to* KAMEV] Quiet, Comrade. Or you will find yourself in my report.

KAMEV: Report?

MOKHOVA: You could get into a lot of trouble.

KAMEV: For what?

MOKHOVA: For being in my report.

KAMEV: I haven't done anything.

MOKHOVA: Be quiet, Comrade!

KAMEV: I'm not the one discussing Meyerhold with my boyfriend.

MOKHOVA: Yes, but you are discussing Meyerhold with me and that's enough.

KAMEV: Yes, but that's only to—

MOKHOVA: 'Today, the actor L.G. Kamev discussed the work of counter-revolutionary artist and people's enemy V.E. Meyerhold.'

KAMEV: That's a complete lie!

MOKHOVA: No, Comrade, it is an incomplete truth.

KAMEV: You want me arrested?

MOKHOVA: No, Comrade, I want you to shut up! Can you do that?

KAMEV: [*moving back upstage to sulk and examine his wounds*] Denouncing me! Denouncing me!

MOKHOVA: Nadia, we need to know. Can you help?

NADIA: Help?

MOKHOVA: Speak to someone about Trifinov?

NADIA: Oh, no, dear, no.

KLIMENKO: Come on, Nadia. Everyone knows you have pull.

NADIA: Klimenko, please don't make me sound like a draughthorse.

MOKHOVA: This is an emergency. You can make the call now from the backstage phone. At least find out if he has been taken?

NADIA: Of course he has been taken. He has hardly been delayed by the tram system, has he?

YAKONOVA: Oh, God!

MOKHOVA: Everyone, please, let us please remain calm. It still may be nothing, a delay of some sort. Maybe you can use the same channels. We need to find out.

KLIMENKO: Same channels as who? Have you been asking for special favours, Comrade Stage Manager?

MOKHOVA: No!

BABELEV: Sounds suspiciously against regulations to me.

KLIMENKO: It's always the bolshy ones that are the worst offenders.

KAMEV: Pass over your report, Mokhova, we'll add your name to it.

MOKHOVA: It is not what you think.

KLIMENKO: Hey, who are we to condemn you if you use a bit of pull now and then—

MOKHOVA: My father was taken last year. He did nothing wrong, nothing. He was the electrician at the Meyerhold. He hung lanterns. He switched the lights on, he switched them off. That's all he did his entire life, a blameless life, a good man, a Party man, and there was a dreadful mistake. Nadia knows someone in the Kremlin, who's helping us.

NADIA: Now that's enough…

BABELEV: She hasn't been calling her Uncle Joe?

MOKHOVA: No, Molotova.

> KLIMENKO *gives a low whistle.*

NADIA: No, dear, no. This is not done. You must—

KAMEV: Polina Molotova?

KLIMENKO: Now, that's pull! I knew you were connected, Nadia darling, but bloody hell! She has cocktails with Molotov!

MOKHOVA: We have traced my father to a camp near Novosibirsk. She's trying to get him released.

KLIMENKO: We shouldn't hang about, then. She should give old Molotova a call right now. Get the ball rolling.

NADIA: I do not roll balls, young man—No, no, it's too early.

MOKHOVA: Just to find out if he's been taken.

NADIA: No, no, no. It's too much.

MOKHOVA: Just ask Molotova to make inquiries.

NADIA: What good would that do?

MOKHOVA: Because she found my father and she's helping us—

NADIA: [*snapping*] She did not find your father and she's of no help at all. No. I'm sorry. I'm sorry, child. Molotova is quite useless.

MOKHOVA: What do you mean?

NADIA: Molotova knows nothing. It seems. All the Kremlin wives have fallen out of favour. It's impossible. To be perfectly honest, I do not know where your father is.

MOKHOVA: You lied.

NADIA: She lied to me, *to me*. She told me your father was transported and I believed her. But Stalin put an end to those sorts of enquiries months ago, apparently. So she spun me a story.

MOKHOVA: [*stunned*] How long have you known?

NADIA: A few weeks, merely. Who would crush your hopes, dear? [*Pause.*] Poor Molotova, she's very distressed. [*Pause.*] I'm caught between you both. [*Pause.*] I'm sorry. I'm dreadfully sorry. I mean, it doesn't change very much, dear, if you think about it. We had the name of a camp and now we do not. He is more than likely in a prison camp *somewhere*. [*Pause. With embarrassed vehemence*] Why do people insist on importuning me? Why? Taking advantage of an old woman. [*Turning on* KLIMENKO] You! What do you want of me? We may as well have it now, in front of everyone. This big favour. You would like to use my pull. Yes? Take advantage of me. Go ahead. What is it? A better apartment? A job for a nephew? Or to get some black market colleague pulled from prison? What? What?

KLIMENKO: No—

NADIA: What?!

KLIMENKO: Bootlaces.

NADIA: What?

KLIMENKO: I need bootlaces. I have three pairs of street boots that don't have laces. There's none to be had. I heard you can get them at the Party store. That's all. I'd pay you for them.

A long silence. NADIA *takes a seat.* MOKHOVA *has gone to her lectern and is quiet.* YAKONOVA *is recovering.* KAMEV *is upstage in a funk.* DINSKY *takes control.*

DINSKY: Scene seven, then? Is that where we're going from?

KLIMENKO: [*getting into position*] Yeah, let's do something.

DINSKY: Stalin has entered. You are up next to me, Kamev. Kamev?

KAMEV: I will read from here.

DINSKY: Fair enough. Glemov, you're playing, aren't you?

GLEMOV: Sure.

DINSKY: Anyone else want to join us centre stage?

> *No reply.*

So it's everyone throw in lines from where they are? Right-o. So: **Enter Stalin**. The next line is mine. Are you ready, Glemov?

GLEMOV: [*with his script*] Oh, yes. Do you want my accent?

DINSKY: Ah, I don't think the mood is quite right for it. If you would like to save it for Wednesday. [*Reading*] **Oh, Comrade Stalin, you are just in time to settle this little contretemps.**

> GLEMOV *pulls out his pipe.*

GLEMOV: [*his reading is a little stilted but not too bad*] **Now what do we have here?**

DINSKY: **A case of potato pilfering.** [*Pause.*] Your line, Red Army Commander Two.

KAMEV: [*from where he sits, flatly*] **And we suspect a little kiss pilfering into the bargain.**

NADIA: [*rising, getting into position*] **The scamp stole me patatas!**

GLEMOV: **I see. Madam, we have had run-ins with this young man before.**

NADIA: **A hooligan, that's what he is!**

> YAKONOVA *takes up her script and moves into position. During the following, so does* KAMEV. *From a slow start, and despite themselves, the actors are being drawn into the play.* MOKHOVA *moves to her lectern.*

GLEMOV: **I am sure you are right. And believe me, Madam, I will spare no mercy. Comrade!**

KLIMENKO: **Yes, Commander!**

GLEMOV: **On the evidence of this unimpeachable witness, you have been found guilty of theft.**

KLIMENKO: **Commander?**

GLEMOV: **Admit to your crime and your punishment will be light.**

KLIMENKO: **But, Commander...**

GLEMOV: **Let us say, a three-hour detail picking this woman's potatoes. With this young girl to oversee the job. I think it is in your best interest to come clean.**

KLIMENKO: **Maybe, I did steal one potato, Commander.**

YAKONOVA: **Yes he did! I saw him!**

NADIA: **I knew it! The young scamp, I'll box his ears!**

GLEMOV: **Now, now now! What is your name, miss?**

YAKONOVA: **Maria.**

GLEMOV: **Maria, take your prisoner away! And make sure you guard him closely.**

YAKONOVA: **Yes, I will. Thank you, Comrade.**

MOKHOVA: [*back on the book*] **They exit.**

    KAMEV *is on his feet and has come down.*

KAMEV: **You handled that like the perfect diplomat, Comrade.**

DINSKY: **You have the common touch.**

GLEMOV: **Dealing with simple people is simple. It is second guessing the crafty wiles of the intelligent that requires true diplomacy.**

KAMEV: **It didn't go well?**

GLEMOV: **Trotsky wants us to pick up sticks and head north to repel the Polish counterattack.**

DINSKY: **But that's madness! Absolute madness! The fight is here.**

GLEMOV: **I am afraid Trotsky has twisted the ear of Lenin.**

KAMEV: **Do they want us to lose the war?**

GLEMOV: **Perhaps.**

DINSKY: **What do you mean?**

GLEMOV: **Don't you perceive his cunning? Trotsky wants us in the northern front so that when the defeat comes—and it will—he will have the First Cavalry to blame.**

DINSKY: **That's outrageous!**

KAMEV: **How can Lenin listen to him? It is clear to everyone that Stalin is a treacherous dog!**

GLEMOV: **Now, now, Comrade. He's more of a wily fox, and we must be smarter to outwit him. For he**— [*He tentatively stops the reading.*] Excuse me, but that can't be right.

DINSKY: No, you were very good, wasn't he, everyone? For your first time.

GLEMOV: No, I mean that line, it can't be right.

BABELEV: Which line?

GLEMOV: Just now. Kamev's line. Just sounded wrong to me.

KAMEV: Don't worry, young friend. We often get that feeling reading Comrade Babelev's lines.

MOKHOVA: All right, can we have the line again?

GLEMOV: A couple of lines back.

KAMEV: An actor, then a playwright, and now a critic—all in the space of a day.

DINSKY: A theatrical prodigy! Good for you, Glemov!

GLEMOV: Sorry, I—I might be wrong. It was just—it sounded—wrong.

BABELEV: Just give us the line again.

KAMEV: Well, which one? **Do they want us to lose the war?**

GLEMOV: No, later.

KAMEV: **How can Lenin listen to him? It is clear to everyone that Stalin is a treacherous dog!**

GLEMOV: That line.

There are blank stares from one to another as everyone tries to see what the error is. A long silence.

BABELEV: Yeah, yeah, yeah, what's wrong with it?

KAMEV: Oh, let's press on.

GLEMOV: No, but, surely…

MOKHOVA: Are we moving on?

GLEMOV: Just say it one more time, please.

BABELEV: One more time, Kamev.

KAMEV: And then we move on? **How can Lenin listen to him? It is clear to everyone that Stalin is a treacherous dog!**

GLEMOV: There!

KAMEV: Yes?

BABELEV: What?

GLEMOV: Don't you mean 'Trotsky'?

> *Another long silence, but this time with a dawning horror from everyone.*

BABELEV: Oh, n-n-n-no, no, no, no, no, no, no, that can't be right!

KAMEV: My God, Babelev! What words have you put into my mouth?

BABELEV: I didn't. I didn't. It must have been the typists. They're always making mistakes.

KAMEV: You had me calling Stalin a treacherous dog.

BABELEV: Yeah, yeah, yeah, just…

KAMEV: To his face.

BABELEV: Calm down, will you?

KAMEV: On his birthday!

BABELEV: There's four months of rehearsals, Kamev. We would have caught it long before opening night. It's a typist mistake!

MOKHOVA: It's here in your manuscript.

BABELEV: [*moving around to her lectern*] Where? Where?

GLEMOV: I didn't mean to get anyone into trouble.

BABELEV: [*looking at the book*] Shit! Shit! I was writing like a fury last night. Shit!

NADIA: [*the swearing*] Please, Babelev, you're in the theatre.

> BABELEV *snatches the offending page from* MOKHOVA*'s hand.*

BABELEV: Give that to me!

MOKHOVA: Comrade, hand that back!

BABELEV: I am just reclaiming what is mine.

MOKHOVA: It is not yours. It is the Company's. Hand it back!

BABELEV: I will write it out again. No-one will know. I'll burn them. [*The cast's pages*] I will take those as well.

> BABELEV *goes from person to person in turn taking or snatching away from each their incriminating page. Only* KAMEV *shows any resistance.*

KAMEV: Are you trying to kill me, Babelev?

BABELEV: Just hand the page over.

KAMEV: [*folding the page and moving away*] What if one of the stagehands had heard me saying that line?

BABELEV: Hand it over.

MOKHOVA: Just give him the page and we'll move on.

KLIMENKO: Yeah, let's just forget about it.

KAMEV: [*folding the page and placing it in his jacket pocket*] And what if I don't want to forget about it?

BABELEV: Give me the fucking page!

NADIA: Gentleman! The theatre!

DINSKY: Come on, chum. Just hand it over. Innocent mistake and all that. No bones broken.

BABELEV: [*throwing up his hands*] Keep it, then, keep it, Kamev. If you really want it. Frame it, put it up on your dressing-room wall. Whatever you like. I don't care.

> BABELEV *lunges suddenly at* KAMEV, *catching him off guard.* BABELEV *has a hand in* KAMEV*'s jacket. There is a brief struggle.*

KAMEV: Ahh! Stop it! Get out of there! No, no. I'll give it to you! I'll give it to you!

> BABELEV *pulls out not one but two paper items, the incriminating page and an envelope.*

BABELEV: Thank you very much. And to show there's no hard feelings, I'll mail your letter for you too [*reading the address*] —to the District Commissar of the NKVD.

KAMEV: Give it back.

BABELEV: Conducting a little police business, are you?

KAMEV: That has nothing to do with you. Just hand it back.

BABELEV: [*moving away to take the letter out of the envelope and peruse it*] Oh, surprise! A letter of denunciation!

KAMEV: It's private, Babelev.

KLIMENKO: Are you a spy, Kamev?

KAMEV: No, of course not.

BABELEV: [*reading*] 'I, Leon Grigoryevich Kamev, a theatre worker in Moscow and a good Communist…' You, a good Communist?

KLIMENKO: He's a better actor than we thought.

BABELEV: Just look, three pages of names. Who are these people? I don't know any of these names.

> KLIMENKO *takes the list.*

KAMEV: It is an old list. Useless. Give it back.

KLIMENKO: I know this guy. Smirenski. Runs the theatre down in Kherson.

DINSKY: You denounced Smirenski?

KAMEV: I haven't denounced anyone. The letter was in my pocket. Give it back.

KLIMENKO: [*glancing down the page*] And L.V. Kaverin—that's not Lev, is it? Who was he with?

NADIA: The Vakhtangov under Popov. I haven't heard word of him for years.

DINSKY: He was with us in Odessa. Kamev, what's this about?

KLIMENKO: But I know these names. The last dozen on your list. Trifinov, Babelev…

BABELEV: You bastard, Kamev.

NADIA: Now, let's keep this civil.

KLIMENKO: And, guess what? N.I. Shilovskya…

KAMEV: Look, everyone…

NADIA: What is it that I am supposed to have done?

KLIMENKO: [*reading*] 'Used your Party influence improperly with respect to petitioning the release of enemy of the State A.G. Mokhov.'

MOKHOVA: You shit, Kamev!

NADIA: No, darling, he is an absolute and utter fucker!

KAMEV: There are no secrets in the theatre, you know that.

> BABELEV *moves threateningly towards* KAMEV.

BABELEV: Come clean, Kamev. Are you on spying us?

KAMEV: No! Listen to me.

KLIMENKO: Hey, maybe this has something to do with our director being late.

KAMEV: What?

BABELEV: Is it, Kamev?

KAMEV: No! No! The letter was still in my pocket!

BABELEV: Who have you snitched to?

> BABELEV *begins pushing* KAMEV *hard.* DINSKY *intervenes.*

DINSKY: Now, now, come on. Let's calm down. Please, Babelev. Babelev. Please. This doesn't solve anything. Please.

> BABELEV *pulls back a little.*

BABELEV: Maybe we should denounce *him*. Get up a petition against *him*.

DINSKY: This is the theatre and we are part of the theatrical family. No-one should be denouncing anyone.

KLIMENKO: He's denounced you.

DINSKY: What?

KLIMENKO: You're on here. You're 'an unrepentant follower of Meyerhold'.

> DINSKY *takes the letter and reads his denouncement.*

KAMEV: I was never going to—

DINSKY: [*utterly bewildered*] Why?

KAMEV: I just keep it. I don't know why I do.

DINSKY: I haven't worked for Meyerhold for years, you know that. You know that. You know that because I have been by your side. Next to you and Rula.

KAMEV: It is just something I keep. Since Rula. Because I don't... because Rula had such spirit. You know that, Dinsky, such spirit.

DINSKY: [*the letter*] Yes, but this.

KAMEV: I was sure they were going to take me.

DINSKY: [*suddenly angry*] But this!

KAMEV: I don't have her spirit, Dinsky. You know what a wreck I was. I thought, when they come for me, I must have something. Because interrogation... I don't have her spirit. She must have spat in their faces, those sons of bitches, screamed the place down. You know that. But me... So I wrote down a few names. That I would give them. Off the bat.

KLIMENKO: A few names?

KAMEV: It was during the purge. Half of them had been taken already and the rest I put together from theatre gossip, things I heard, that were probably true in any case. You know what it was like in Odessa when the purge was on, Dinsky? When I wasn't picked up it was a sort of miracle. So the list became a talisman. I'd have it in my pocket and touch it for good luck. I thought that if I had it ready, there, I would never need to use it, that nothing could happen to me.

DINSKY: But I got us out of Odessa. *I did.* I got you out of that hole. Got you back to Moscow.

KAMEV: Yes, I know, and I put it away once we returned to Moscow. But when they went after Meyerhold I pulled it out again. Just to keep the fear at bay. And I freshened it up with some new names.

DINSKY: But mine.

KAMEV: It just occurred to me that yours had to be there. It didn't seem a genuine denunciation unless I denounced you, Dinsky. My best and oldest friend.

DINSKY: You are contemptible.

KAMEV: [*with sudden anger*] A death certificate in the morning post! That's all I got. That's all! They didn't even give me back her body!

> *Silence.* DINSKY *folds up the letter and takes the envelope from* BABELEV. *He places the letter back into the envelope, gives it to* KAMEV *and goes quietly upstage.*

BABELEV: You can remove my name, arsehole. You can remove everybody's name.

KAMEV: [*ripping up the list*] There! There! There! Gone!

KLIMENKO: Yeah, but what is to prevent him from making another list?

KAMEV: I won't!

YAKONOVA: I'll find myself on the new list, for sure. Just for upstaging him.

KAMEV: You have my word. My denouncing career is over. I won't.

DINSKY: [*softly*] Yes, you would, Kamev.

KAMEV: Dinsky, I swear.

DINSKY: It makes no difference whether you keep a denunciation in your pocket or not. Or if it is you, or if it is me, or anyone else. If they snatch you, you will denounce all the same, denounce who they want you to denounce, say what they want you to say. We all know that.

MOKHOVA: [*a warning by reflex*] Comrade...

DINSKY: That's reportable, isn't it? Bugger, bugger, bum, bum.

MOKHOVA: I will have nothing to report today.

DINSKY: Good for you. Take the day off. Maybe we should all take the day off. Take the day off from being artists of the Soviet Theatre. For once be real in life and keep the pretence for the stage. For God's sake, theatre's not that important.

YAKONOVA: I think it's important.

DINSKY: Larrisa, when you are young you think everything is important. When I started out, my director at that time used to go on about the future we were building with our art. And young idealist that I was, I went with it. And I remember I was performing on the gangway of this set, one of those constructivist jobs of Popova's.

BABELEV: Is this with M?

DINSKY: Yes, yes, it was a production of Vsevelod Emiliovich Meyerhold! There—a counter-revolutionary act. Who's going to turn me in?

MOKHOVA: Go ahead, Dinsky.

DINSKY: Anyway, there were a dozen of us all in bright blue boilersuits and goggles, doing synchronised movement to some music from a firemen's band.

KLIMENKO: Formalistic crap.

DINSKY: It wasn't crap! That was the surprising thing. It was rather wonderful. You could see the faces of the audience upturned towards you, staring in wonder at the spectacle. And it occurred to me that afterwards they weren't going home talking about the stuff Meyerhold drummed into us, the Party line about the corruption of bourgeois values on the... you know, that stuff. They were going to go home talking about the set and the costumes and this bit, and that bit, and that joke, and the way Illisky's character, who was in love, clambered up the scaffolding like a joyful monkey.

NADIA: I saw that. I still remember it.

KAMEV: [*softly*] Yes. Yes.

DINSKY: And that's theatre, that's all. Not that important, really, but…
What do you want? You laugh a little, you cry a little; who knows?
You might even get to think a little. Meyerhold, I loved the man,
but God he could bang on! Always on his soapbox. even before the
Revolution. And forget the forces of Capitalism, the big enemy was
always Stanislavski and the Moscow Art chaps.

> *Jumping on the rehearsal table, gradually* DINSKY *becomes*
> MEYERHOLD, *the light gradually closing in on his figure (see
> performance note below).*

He'd tell us—and Meyerhold had this intensity when he got going—
Stanislavski's Realism is a keyhole that the Master deigns to let you
peep through. And the audience is a privileged voyeur on a scene
of—a family dinner, let's say. And we are supposed to marvel at how
true-to-life everything is. Look at the wallpaper and the cruet set,
such telling detail! And don't they look just like a family at dinner?
Oh, those delicate, subtle little performances. Such observation!
What art! [*Pause.*] But it's a sham! Because they are all sitting at one
side of the table! And they are all speaking loudly, because they are
not people having dinner, they're actors who must be seen and heard!
You know, Stanislavski liked to say, 'A character's entire world can
collapse while seated at dinner'. Yes, but how does he show it? An
actor's fork stops before his blank face. A teacup rattles softly in her
saucer! But that is not what your world collapsing is like. It feels like a
collapse! A catastrophe cannot be contained in a keyhole. When your
world is being destroyed everything slows down; you see nothing,
hear nothing; everything flies away, leaving you in darkness, alone
with your own horror. We feel crushed, knocked off our feet, that's
what we say, isn't it? Because that is what we feel! The reality is the
metaphor, not the pissy little actor's giveaway. The teacup rattles!
God! Who cares! Because the reality is the scream!

> *And* DINSKY / MEYERHOLD *screams. Blackout on* DINSKY.

◆ ◆ ◆ ◆ ◆

Performance Note: From DINSKY *'s speech above, the play transforms swiftly and completely into the sort of non-naturalistic performance that Meyerhold might have directed in the 1920s. This brief, episodic play-within-the-play is* The Tragedy of Meyerhold. *It is important that no attempt be made to 'frame' the action; for example, by suggesting that it is a 'dream sequence' or an improvisation by the actors. It just happens. The major changes are as follows:*

The cast take up the various parts as specified. The performances become 'presentational' rather than natural, and should include choreographed movement, ideally based on Meyerhold's biomechanical principles and études. Extra performers may be used if available.

The set becomes constructivist, with platforms, stairways, ramps and even moving parts. The old set of the refectory and factory disappear. There is a cyclorama or screen at the rear.

The lighting should support the heightened reality or unreality: shadows thrown up on the cyclorama, slides of episode titles and slogans, and historical images of Meyerhold, Raikh, his productions, etcetera, can be used.

Music and other sound effects should be added to support the various rhythms of the action.

Props and costumes appear as needed; a number of props are trick props and will require special manufacture. In all these matters, the stage directions that follow are only a guide.

General: Many of the effects stated below have been created with a large, well-resourced, modern stage in mind. Effects can be achieved much more modestly. Provided they maintain the shape of the story, directors and designers are encouraged to adapt this sequence to the resources available to them. The central thing is the stark contrast between this section and the rest of the play.

EPISODE ONE

Projected title: 'THE TRAGEDY OF MEYERHOLD'

Music: A bright scherzo, early twentieth century.

YAKONOVA / REVOLUTIONARY *enters, crossing the stage in a biomechanical run. She holds a red flag on a stick.*

She stops downstage centre in a running stance.

BOLSHEVIKS *enter with a banner and a large portrait of Lenin.*

BABELEV / BOLSHEVIK *regards* YAKONOVA.

Projected title: 'REVOLUTION'

BABELEV / BOLSHEVIK: Comrades, the Soviet Union is a new society and for it we need a new citizen. Here stands a model for the future. Note how the back is bent for work, the limbs sprung for action, the face intelligent, the mind alert, the eyes set on our radiant future.

> *There is a rumbling sound that quickly builds.*

With this new citizenry we can move forward in a spirit of fraternity, freedom and— [*he stops, wonders what the sound is, then continues*] —and... egalitarianism. No longer will one class exploit another. [*He raises his voice over the din.*] Today, we will work for our own future. What the hell is that?!

> *There is a blast of music and out of the darkness, rolling like a juggernaut, comes a constructivist set, a multi-layered machine with platforms, ramps, stairs, ladders, etcetera. On the top platform, like a captain on the bridge, stands* DINSKY / MEYERHOLD. *Note: The former set of the factory is gone.*

DINSKY / MEYERHOLD: Bolsheviks! The Meyerhold Theatre has joined your revolution!

> YAKONOVA / REVOLUTIONARY *takes off. She runs up the various stairs, ramps and platforms to plant her red flag on the top.*

Comrades, embrace a brother-in-arms. For we have fought the same good fight. We have each wiped away illusions. The Party has overcome the bourgeoisie and I have overcome the bourgeois theatre. You smashed reality and I smashed Realism. Comrades, embrace me!

BABELEV / BOLSHEVIK: [*the construction*] We're not embracing anyone until you tell us what that is?

DINSKY / MEYERHOLD: This? This is a futuristic machine for putting man into space! Comrades, in a radical act my theatre has exploded the box! I have smashed through Stanislavski's three-walled prison and released the actors. On this construction an actor is finally free—free to roam, run, climb, crawl, cry, leap, fight, speak, shout, laugh, swing, kick, kill and love.

KLIMENKO / BOLSHEVIK: That's all very well, Meyerhold, but what does it do?

DINSKY / MEYERHOLD: Do? Why, it does nothing, which is why it can do anything. It represents nowhere which is why it can represent anywhere. The new Soviet Union is sheer potential and so is this stage. The Soviet future and what I present here can only be fully created by using our imaginations. Only on this setting is a truly proletarian theatre possible.

BABELEV / BOLSHEVIK: Your ideology seems sound. Embrace us!

KLIMENKO / BOLSHEVIK: Here, have my worker's cap.

BABELEV / BOLSHEVIK: And try out this cloth coat.

KLIMENKO / BOLSHEVIK: Now lift him into his worker's boots.

> *All lift* DINSKY / MEYERHOLD *above their heads and drop him into a pair of boots.*

We'll get laces for them later.

> DINSKY / MEYERHOLD *walks around in his new costume, enjoying the feel of it.*

DINSKY / MEYERHOLD: Comrades, the construction needs a finishing touch.

> DINSKY / MEYERHOLD *takes the portrait of Lenin and it is passed hand to hand to the top of the construction. They clap and cheer, and the celebration turns into a dance.*
>
> *Peasant dance music.*
>
> *The dance evolves into biomechanical movements.*

The lighting throws giant shadows on the cyclorama.
The music turns into something atonal and strange.

EPISODE TWO

Projected title: '*PEOPLE'S ARTIST*'

The actors turn and perform a biomechanical 'dactyl' that then turns into applause as DINSKY / MEYERHOLD *enters.*

ACTORS: Bravo! Bravo!

DINSKY / MEYERHOLD: All right, enough, enough.

YAKONOVA / RAIKH: I told them, Vsevolod Emilevich, that you didn't want any fuss.

MOKHOVA / ACTOR: It is a great honour: People's Artist!

The actors begin cheering and clapping again.

DINSKY / MEYERHOLD: Yes, yes, it is a great honour which I share with you all. A tribute to all the hard work that we have all done in the name of Soviet Culture. But we artists are not sustained by prizes but by our art. So back to work. Now—come here, Zina—we will demonstrate a new étude. It is called 'Stab with the Dagger'.

Facing each other, DINSKY / MEYERHOLD *and* YAKONOVA / RAIKH *perform the opening dactyl. The lights fade quickly on them.*

EPISODE THREE

Projected title: '*AN ARTISTIC DEBATE*'

A music of mechanical and factory sounds with percussion and steam hissings.

Slides of various Meyerhold productions of the 1920s, including The Magnanimous Cuckold, The Forest, The Bathhouse *and* The Government Inspector.

Lights up on two WORKERS *(*KAMEV *and* GLEMOV*) on the construction. They are engaged in rhythmic factory work, moving simple levers, pullies and wheels, etcetera, that are either fixtures on the set or mimed.*

The movement should look similar to the biomechanical movements at the end of the first episode. They each have different movements or the same movements in a different sequence, coming together to synchronise a pulling across of a large lever which is synchronised with changing slides.

GLEMOV / WORKER: I loved it!

KAMEV / WORKER: [*disbelieving*] You loved it?

GLEMOV / WORKER: I loved it. Brilliant!

KAMEV / WORKER: Brilliant?

GLEMOV / WORKER: Brilliant. Funny.

KAMEV / WORKER: Funny?

GLEMOV / WORKER: Very funny. Imaginative.

KAMEV / WORKER: Imaginative? Big word.

GLEMOV / WORKER: Imaginative.

KAMEV / WORKER: For you.

GLEMOV / WORKER: Piss off!

KAMEV / WORKER: No, I am just saying that Meyerhold must have come up with something pretty bloody good to inspire an unskilled Moscow factory hand who can barely write his own name to such flights of verbal expressionism.

GLEMOV / WORKER: Well, I loved it. And so did the wife and her mother.

KAMEV / WORKER: Ah, the rank and file comrades have delivered their critical verdict, have they? But I tell you, I have seen plays at the Meyerhold, and frankly I found them far too clever for the likes of me. If I had my way—

He stops and looks up to the cyclorama where the current slide is out of focus.

Hold on, trouble!

In unison, they begin cranking at a wheel and the indistinguishable blur slowly resolves into the face of Stalin.

EPISODE FOUR

Projected title: '*THE VISIT OF THE COMMISSARS*'

Some light comic entry music.

Three COMMISSARS *(*NADIA, BABELEV, KLIMENKO*) enter. They move and act as one, though* NADIA *is the head. Their smiles are fixed.*

NADIA / HEAD COMMISSAR: [*very rapidly and crisply*] I assume that you are aware of the new policy that Soviet art should depict the reality of life as it is lived today in the Soviet Union.

DINSKY / MEYERHOLD: Of course, I am aware—

NADIA / HEAD COMMISSAR: So why aren't we seeing it in your work? You have received repeated warnings about Meyerholdism.

DINSKY / MEYERHOLD: To be honest I am not quite clear what Meyerholdism is.

NADIA / HEAD COMMISSAR: I don't think it is the job of a humble Commissar of the Artist Affairs Department to tell the great Meyerhold what Meyerholdism is.

BABELEV / COMMISSAR: It is what you do.

NADIA / HEAD COMMISSAR: And we want you to stop doing it.

KLIMENKO / COMMISSAR: Vsevolod Emilevich, just give us a plainly-told tale about Soviet citizens overcoming the odds and the forces of reaction.

BABELEV / COMMISSAR: With a romantic angle, boy and a girl.

NADIA / HEAD COMMISSAR: And a tractor.

BABELEV / COMMISSAR: And uplift.

DINSKY / MEYERHOLD: Well, the play that we will preview for you today is our attempt at the official style. I hope you will like it.

NADIA / HEAD COMMISSAR: Oh, we hope we do, too, Vsevolod Emilevich.

> *The* COMMISSARS *sit downstage facing the audience, their smiles still fixed. What they watch is performed in shadow play or mime on the construction behind them.*
>
> *Sound: The lines of the play in a comically heightened Russian or Russian-sounding gobbledygook.*
>
> *The* COMMISSARS *react in stages in unison:*
>
> *1. With attention.*
> *2. Interested, they lean in.*

3. *Curious. They lean in further.*

4. *They lean in further still.*

5. *They pull back with alarm.*

6 *Their smiles disappear.*

7. *In distaste, they lean back.*

8. *In revulsion, they lean back further, holding up their hands to block out the sight.*

9. *They turn their heads away.*

NADIA / HEAD COMMISSAR: [*shaking her head vigorously*] No, no, no!

OTHER COMMISSARS: [*shaking their heads*] No, no, no!

> *Projected caption: 'FORMALISM!'*

> *Sound: The play stops.*

> *The shadow play stops and the shadows stand around bemused. The* COMMISSARS *stand and begin to exit.* DINSKY / MEYERHOLD *enters.*

DINSKY / MEYERHOLD: [*desperately*] Comrades, please, please. There are still two acts to go. Let's just stop and talk about it for a minute.

> DINSKY / MEYERHOLD *runs after the* COMMISSARS, *who move away in slow motion.*

> DINSKY / MEYERHOLD *doesn't get anywhere with his running. His arms and limbs begin to flail but the more furiously he chases, the wider the distance opens up between them.*

> *The shadows on the cyclorama reach out towards the departing* COMMISSARS, *becoming an anemone of arms.*

> DINSKY / MEYERHOLD *trips and falls as the* COMMISSARS *disappear into the wings.*

EPISODE FIVE

Projected title: 'AN ALIEN THEATRE'

KAMEV / ACTOR *is discovered sitting in a chair facing the wings. He has opened a copy of* Pravda *and he is flipping through it. He sees an article and becomes alarmed.*

KAMEV / ACTOR: [*calling out*] Hey, here, quickly! They're writing about Vsevolod Emilevich in *Pravda*.

> *One by one, other Meyerhold* ACTORS *come across. They eventually form a tight group that leans precariously—impossibly—over* KAMEV / ACTOR'*s shoulder to read the article.*

[*Reading*] 'On the occasion of the twentieth anniversary of the Great Socialist Revolution only one out of the seven hundred Soviet professional theatres was without a special production to commemorate the event. That theatre was Meyerhold's theatre.'

NADIA / ACTOR: 'It has become absolutely clear that Meyerhold cannot and, apparently, will not comprehend Soviet reality…'

GLEMOV / ACTOR: '… or depict the problems that concern every Soviet citizen.'

MOKHOVA / ACTOR: 'His systematic deviation from Soviet reality…'

BABELEV / ACTOR: '… his political distortions…'

KAMEV / ACTOR: Oh, that's bad: 'distortions'

KLIMENKO / ACTOR: '… his political distortions and hostile slanders…'

YAKONOVA / ACTOR: '… have brought his theatre…'

BABELEV / ACTOR: '… to total…'

MOKHOVA / ACTOR: '… ideological…'

GLEMOV / ACTOR: '… and artistic…'

NADIA / ACTOR: '… ruin…'

YAKONOVA / ACTOR: '… and…'

KLIMENKO / ACTOR: '… shameful…'

KAMEV / ACTOR: '… bankruptcy.'

ALL: 'Do Soviet art and the Soviet public really need such a theatre?'

NADIA / ACTOR: Oh, dear me, that sounded like a rhetorical question!

> *The* ACTORS *look around fearfully. The light suddenly snaps into darkness with a terrible finality.*

EPISODE SIX

Projected title: '*ALL-UNION CONFERENCE OF THEATRE DIRECTORS, MOSCOW 1939*'

DINSKY / MEYERHOLD *is at a lectern on the upper level of the set. Eventually taking a stance behind him is a smiling* KLIMENKO / COMMISSAR.

DINSKY / MEYERHOLD: [*speaking slowly and haltingly*] I would like to begin this address to the Directors' Conference by paying my respects to…

> *The lectern begins to shake and the shaking increases throughout the speech.*

… Comrade General Secretary Joseph Stalin, our leader and mentor; a friend and inspiration to oppressed workers throughout the world.

> *A sheet of his speech drops from the lectern.*

He is the great teacher from whom we learn our lessons and who points out our mistakes.

> *More papers fly from the lectern.*

He also grants the Soviet Artist the opportunity when his mistakes are especially grave, as mine have been…

> *The lectern is now shaking violently, spilling great quantities of paper.*

… to admit those mistakes to a gathering of my peers, such as this…

> *He stops to cough and everything goes still.*

… and to dedicate himself to their correction.

> DINSKY / MEYERHOLD *coughs again.*
>
> *At the bottom of the set an arm thrusts through the construction. In the hand is the 'poisoned' teacup from Act One. A spotlight follows the teacup as, one by one, disembodied arms thrusting out from the construction pass it up towards* DINSKY / MEYERHOLD.
>
> KLIMENKO / COMMISSAR *finally takes it and holds it out to* DINSKY / MEYERHOLD, *who in the manner of* DINSKY*'s demonstration in Act One, drinks. He passes the cup back.*

Thank you… and to dedicate himself to their correction. Comrade Stalin is the kindly teacher who, at the end of the school day when you have been forgetful, wipes your slate clean.

EPISODE SEVEN

Projected caption: '*A SCENE FROM MACBETH*'

Sound: The two handclaps of the biomechanical dactyl, repeated with long silences in between.

KLIMENKO / COMMISSAR *leads* DINSKY / MEYERHOLD, *who is in a kind of daze, down to the lower platform, where there is a black cubicle.*

DINSKY / MEYERHOLD *is pushed back into it to face the audience.*

DINSKY / MEYERHOLD: [*taking all the parts in a small faraway voice*]
    Where is your husband?
    I hope in no place so unsanctified
    Where such as thou may'st find him.
    He is a traitor.
    Thou liest, thou shag-haired villain.
    What, you egg. Young fry of treachery.
    He has killed me, mother; run away, I pray you.

On the construction above, while the lines are spoken, a variation on the biomechanical étude 'Stab with the Dagger' plays out with YAKONOVA / RAIKH *and two* MURDERERS *(*KLIMENKO *and* GLEMOV*). The multiple stabbing ends with two clear stabs to the eyes.*

The body of YAKONOVA / RAIKH *rolls along the platform as she sings a sad peasant song. At the edge, the body falls into the darkness.*

The COMMISSARS *close the door of the box on* DINSKY / MEYERHOLD. *They tip back the box and lift it up onto their shoulders. It is now a coffin. They carry it to the front of the stage and place it down.*

Standing upstage, the COMMISSARS *remove their hats in reverence, then all at once jump up and flatten the coffin.*

EPISODE EIGHT

Projected title: '*A SORT OF FUNERAL*'

A low hum.

The cast (except GLEMOV*) have become themselves again. They are still in their costumes but are now 'out of character'. For this section the acting is naturalistic. Tentatively, they make their way down to the flattened coffin.* DINSKY *joins them. They stand around the coffin at a loss.*

KLIMENKO *lifts up the coffin a few inches and looks underneath, just in case.*

KLIMENKO: Nothing.

KAMEV: They didn't even give us his body.

NADIA: I simply cannot get used to this new Soviet way of doing things.

MOKHOVA: So many arrests and so few trials.

KAMEV: So many deaths and so few funerals.

BABELEV: One more performance banned by the authorities.

MOKHOVA: Poor Meyerhold.

YAKONOVA: And poor Zinaida Raikh.

DINSKY: Yes. And poor Zina. Would anyone else like to remember someone while we have this flattened coffin from the props department?

BABELEV: Well, the poets I loved—now dead or silenced.

YAKONOVA: My professors at university—all but the dullest now dust.

NADIA: My husband's comrades from the Revolution. Had his heart not given way in '33, I suppose Victor would have joined them.

MOKHOVA: I don't want to think about it.

DINSKY: Fair enough. Kamev?

KAMEV: Rula.

DINSKY: Of course.

> KLIMENKO *pulls a letter from his wallet.*

KLIMENKO: [*reading*] 'We are desperate, son. Please. Your brothers have disappeared. To where? God knows. Leaving me with Sacha's three youngest, who are wasting away before me. I have a little money left but there is no food to buy.' Sent from Birky, Poltavska in the Ukraine in December 1932, but not received until the following spring.

NADIA: What can one do?

BABELEV: We can seek justice.

MOKHOVA: Impossible.

KAMEV: Nothing's impossible in the theatre.

YAKONOVA: Meyerhold's Law.

DINSKY: We are still in the realm of wishful thinking.

MOKHOVA: In that case, we will need a villain to punish.

> *On cue, from a trapdoor in the floor behind them, in a cloud of smoke,* GLEMOV *as Stalin rises.*

EPISODE NINE

Projected captions: 'FATHER OF THE SOVIETS', 'THE GREAT TEACHER', 'FRIEND OF TOILERS THROUGHOUT THE WORLD'.

Music builds until the ending.

GLEMOV / STALIN: Comrades, in my big Georgian hand I carry the latest five-year plan, a blueprint for the future…

BABELEV: I wasn't thinking of going so far.

KLIMENKO: Can we place the Terror at his door?

NADIA: He knew about it all. He ordered it all.

DINSKY: Then according to the poetic licence invested in us, I say, arrest him!

> *All grab* GLEMOV / STALIN *and lift him bodily above their heads. The episode has fully reverted to stylisation.*

GLEMOV / STALIN: [*protesting*] But, Comrades, in my big Georgian hand I carry the latest five-year plan, a blueprint for the future…

KAMEV: Let the punishment fit the crime!

BABELEV: Stuff his mouth with dry words!

YAKONOVA: Fill his ears with dead music!

DINSKY: Cram his head with slogans!

NADIA: Oh, let's just hang him!

ALL: Yes!

> *They take him up to the lower platform, where the hook and chain from the factory have been lowered.* YAKONOVA *pulls out a large*

red handkerchief and passes it to KAMEV, *who ties it as a noose around* GLEMOV / STALIN*'s neck and attaches it to the chain.*

GLEMOV / STALIN: Is this justice?!

KAMEV: No, it's better than that: it's catharsis!

The cast gather at the bottom of the platform. MOKHOVA *gives him a kick and he drops.*

On the rope the dead STALIN, *his neck snapped to the side, rises slowly, so that he dangles some way above the cast, who, arms reaching up towards him, hold a tableau.*

ALL: Life has become better! Life has become more cheerful!

The light rapidly closes in to a tight spot on STALIN.

New music begins: the bright, happy scherzo that began the sequence.

To the music, the spotlight drops from STALIN, *down the tableau of bodies to the stage floor and runs down to the apron, where it stops briefly. Then it begins to move along the edge of the stage to the downstage left door, centring on the doorknob. The music stops. A pause. The doorknob rattles, stops, rattles again more strongly. Then there is a furious banging which could be someone trying to unstick the door or authorities demanding attention. A second bang and the door bursts open. It is* TRIFINOV, *late thirties or so.*

TRIFINOV: Hell's frigging bells! Mokhova, get Kostya to have a look at this door. Sorry, everyone, sorry! Sorry, sorry. Grabbed a nap in the props room and overslept, didn't I? Now, let's—

The light broadens, a slow dawning, that reveals the Precision Milled *set as it was. The actors stand in the final tableau with* GLEMOV *dangling above, all now back in rehearsal clothes. They have turned their heads in dumbfounded surprise towards* TRIFINOV.

In his waking torpor, TRIFINOV *tries to work out what is going on. Eventually, he looks at* GLEMOV *dangling from his hook.*

Glemov, you're not due in until Wednesday.

ALL: [*matter-of-factly*] Yes, but the woman below him cooks cabbage.
     The tableau holds as the lights fade to black.

THE END